marie claire
idées

Irresistible Bags

45 contemporary designs for all occasions

quadrille

This edition first published in 2009 by
Quadrille Publishing Limited
Alhambra House
27–31 Charing Cross Road
London WC2H 0LS

Originally published by
Éditions MARIE CLAIRE
10, boulevard des Frères-Voisin,
92130 Issy-Les-Moulineaux Cedex 9 – France

Translation and project management: Anne McDowall
Production: Vincent Smith, Marina Asenjo

British Library Cataloguing-in-Publication Data
A catalogue record for this book is available from the British Library.

ISBN: 978 184400 647 2

Printed in China

NOTES

Some of the templates have been reduced in scale. To find their correct size, enlarge them
on a photocopier until the scale bar on the template shows the measurement indicated.
All fabric measurements given are based on a standard fabric width of 112.5 cm.
Bag sizes given are height x width unless otherwise stated.
The following abbreviations have been used: ch chain, cm centimetre, m metre, mm millimetre,
RS right side, st stitch(es), WS wrong side.

Irresistible Bags

45 contemporary designs for all occasions

Contents

Simply stylish

PASTORAL PRINT BAG
Sizes: 36 x 40 cm (bag); 18 x 12 cm (purse)

MATERIALS
1.2 m of toile de Jouy fabric ● Scissors ● Dylon hot-water fabric dyes: yellow, olive green, purple ● Matching sewing thread ● Ribbon: 80 cm each of 3 different colours for the bag, 30 cm x 4 for the purse + 1.2 m for the purse strap ● Dark red fabric paint ● Paintbrush ● Plain cotton for the lining: 1.2 x 1.2 m for the bag and 30 x 25 cm for the purse ● Pins ● Seed beads ● Fine needle ● Thick piece of cardboard 36 x 9 cm ● Safety pin.

METHOD FOR THE BAG
Following the pattern on page 96, cut out the different pieces – A x 2, B x 1, C x 2 and D x 2 – adding a 1 cm seam allowance all around. You will also need 2 strips of 60 x 6 cm for the handles.

Dye the A pieces and the handles in an equal mixture of yellow and olive green, the B piece in the same colours but in different proportions, and the C piece in purple. Leave to dry, then iron.

With RS facing, sew the various pieces together 1 cm in from the edges (see template for placement). Iron open the seams. Topstitch the C pieces and hand sew the ribbon on the top pieces (A). Following the designs on page 97, paint the flowers freehand on the central section of the bag using fabric paint. Assemble the bag by sewing the side panels to the front and back of the bag, RS together.

Fold over 1 cm down each side of the handles and iron flat. Fold in half lengthways, WS facing, and sew the sides together. Attach a safety pin to one end, and turn RS out.

Cut out the lining in a single piece. With RS together, stitch the side panels to the front and back.

Fold over 1 cm along the top edges of both bag and lining and iron flat. With WS together, slide the lining inside the bag, placing the cardboard in the base between the layers. Pin the handle ends between the bag and lining, 24 cm apart and equidistant from each side. Topstitch the top edge of the bag.

METHOD FOR THE PURSE
Cut out 2 of each pattern piece, adding a 1 cm seam allowance all around. Dye in the colours shown. Cut out the lining in 2 pieces.

With RS facing, sew the various pieces together 1 cm in from the edges. Stitch the ribbon in place along the joins of the purse pieces. With RS facing, sew the front and back of the purse together along the bottom and sides. Make the lining in the same way.

Fold over 1 cm along the top edge of both purse and lining and iron flat. Turn both RS out and slip the lining inside the bag. Tuck the ends of the ribbon strap between the 2 layers at the sides of the purse. Hand stitch the top edges.

Fold the last length of ribbon in 2. Join the edges with 2 or 3 small stitches. Thread the needle and knot the end. Insert it through the ribbon and thread beads to 2.5 cm length, then come up to the ribbon through all the beads. Repeat every 1.5 cm.

(see also pages 96–7)

Simply stylish

FELT EVENING BAG
Size: 25 x 18 cm

MATERIALS

30 x 44 cm of red felt ● Pins ● Scissors ● 39 small round black beads ● Black sewing thread ● Fine needle for sewing on beads and a thicker one for blanket stitch ● DMC stranded embroidery thread in black .

METHOD

Enlarge the design and cut out a template. Pin the template to the felt and cut out 2 pieces. Cut out the hole for the handle.

Sew the beads onto one of the pieces, in clusters of 3 to look like little flowers.

Using black embroidery thread, blanket stitch around the inside edge of each handle and around the top edge of each piece as far as the horizontal notches.

Pin the 2 pieces WS together and, beginning at the level of one horizontal mark and working down and round to the other one, sew both layers together with black blanket stitches.

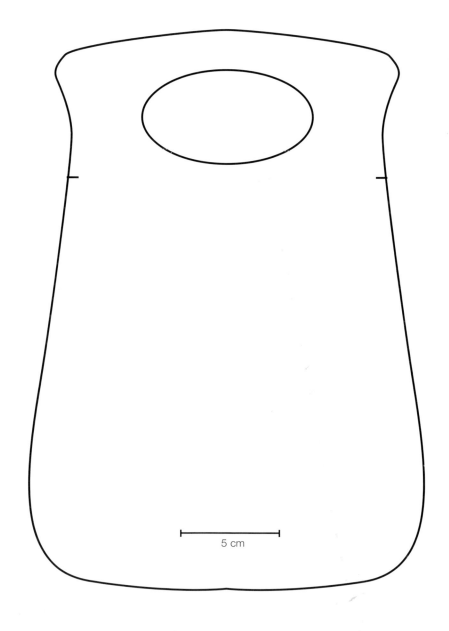

5 cm

Simply stylish

STARS AND CHECKS
Size: 35 x 29 cm

MATERIALS
1 m of tartan silk ● 60 cm of plain-coloured silk ● Scissors ● White fabric-marking pencil ● Embroidery hoop ● Very fine needle ● White sewing thread ● White seed beads ● Pins ● Sewing thread.

METHOD
Cut out 2 rectangles of 42 x 33 cm (which includes 2 cm for the seam allowances and 5 cm for the folded edge at the top) in both the tartan and the plain silk. In the tartan silk only, cut 2 rectangles of 75 x 10 cm for the handles.

Using the photo as a guide, mark the position of the beading on the WS of one of the tartan pieces using the white fabric-marking pencil. Place the fabric in the embroidery hoop and sew on the seed beads for each stitch of the design, juxtaposing several beads for the circles from which the other stars are shooting.

Pin the 2 tartan fabric pieces RS together and stitch the bottom and sides together 2 cm in from the edge. Turn over the top edge by 5 cm and iron flat. Assemble the plain silk lining in the same way.

Fold the handle pieces lengthways with RS together and sew them along their length, leaving the ends open. Turn them RS out and iron. Slip the plain lining into the tartan bag, WS together. Tuck the ends of each handle between the 2 layers of fabric, spacing them about 15 cm apart and equidistant from each side, and pin in place. Topstitch around the top edge of the bag, 1 cm in from the edge.

Simply stylish

EMBROIDERED FLOWERS
Size: approximately 18 cm tall

MATERIALS
40 cm of fuchsia-coloured silk taffeta ● 40 cm of thick iron-on interfacing ● Scissors ● White dressmaker's carbon ● DMC embroidery thread: 1 skein each of very dark parrot green 904, medium light topaz 725, light plum 3607, plum 718 ● 1 m of 15mm-wide dark purple silk ribbon ● Size 9 embroidery needle ● Round-ended size 24 needle for the ribbon ● Small embroidery hoop ● Matching thread ● 1.5 m of fuchsia-coloured suede cord ● Pins.

STITCHES USED
Straight stitch, satin stitch, stem stitch and bullion knot (see page 125).

METHOD
Enlarge the pattern on page 98. Cut 2 of each pattern piece in both the silk taffeta (one for the bag, one for the lining) and the iron-on interfacing, adding a 1 cm seam allowance around each piece.

Trace the floral design on page 99 onto the dressmaker's carbon. With the silk bag piece still folded, transfer the design onto the centre of the fabric. Use coloured thread and ribbon to embroider flowers, following the stitch and colour references shown on the design.

Iron the interfacing onto the WS of all silk pieces. With RS facing, stitch the sides of the bag together.

Cut the cord into 2 equal lengths. Pin one end of both cord pieces to the bottom of one side seam, leaving a 1 cm overhang to sew into the base seam. Then take them up the sides of the bag and pin them to the top. Do the same with the other ends on the opposite side of the bag. The surplus will form the handles.

With RS together, sew the base to the sides of the bag. Turn RS out, then remove the pins.

Make up the lining in the same way as the bag, but leave a 15 cm-wide opening in the side seam. Slide the lining into the bag so that RS are together. Stitch together around the top, then turn RS out. Neatly sew up the opening in the lining and slide it back into the bag.

Straighten the handles and sew them to the top of the bag with a few invisible stitches.

(see also page 98–9)

Simply stylish

TRANSPARENT CHIC
Size: 15 x 15 cm

MATERIALS

**25 cm of tarlatan ● Scissors ●
Needle ● White sewing thread ●
70 cm of 15 mm-wide white
ribbon ● Clear glass droplet
beads.**

METHOD

Cut 2 x 16 cm squares of fabric for
the front and back of the bag and a
strip 48 x 5 cm long for the side
panels and bottom.

Using a zigzag stitch, sew the strip
along 3 sides of one fabric square,
then onto the other. Sew a 5 mm
double hem around the top.

Cut the ribbon in half. Fold the ends
5 mm under and sew onto the top
of each side of the bag, one on
each side, to create handles.

Sew clear glass droplet beads in a
random pattern on the sides of the
bag to look like raindrops.

Simply stylish

SILVER DIAMONDS
Size: 18 x 15 cm

MATERIALS
2 rectangles 20.5 x 17 cm of silver-grey velvet ● 2 rectangles 20.5 x 17 cm of silver-grey lining fabric ● 4.5 m silver sequin string ● Needle and matching thread ● Scissors ● Very fine wire ● Silver-coloured cord.

METHOD
Sew the 2 pieces of velvet together, RS facing, leaving one short side open. Repeat with the lining. Turn the velvet bag RS out.

Lay the sequins onto the front of the bag to form a pattern of diagonals and sew them in place with small invisible stitches.

Slip the lining into the bag (WS together). Turn over the top edges by 5 mm then by 1 cm and hem.

Cut 2 lengths of the wire and 2 of the cord to the size of the desired handles. Thread the wire through the centre of the cord, form into handles and twist each end into a decorative spiral. Sew the handles firmly onto each side of the bag.

Simply stylish

WHIMSICALLY RETRO
Size: 12 x 22 cm

MATERIALS
30 cm each of turquoise linen, white poplin and thin wadding ● Scissors ● Needle and thread ● Dressmaker's carbon ● Pins ● Ballpoint pen ● Thick white nylon thread or silk braid ● White heavy-duty thread ● Press stud.

METHOD
Enlarge the pattern opposite and cut out 2 pieces in each of the 3 fabrics. (Seam allowances are included in the pattern.)

Transfer the design to the linen using dressmaker's carbon. Tack the WS of linen pieces onto the wadding. Machine-stitch the centre and outer contours of the flowers using the heavy-duty thread.

With RS together, sew the 2 pieces of linen together, leaving the top edge open. Do the same with the poplin pieces to make the lining.

To make the bag handle, cut a 35 x 3.5 cm strip of linen. Fold over 1 cm along each length and iron flat, then fold in half lengthways. Stitch along the edge of the handle.

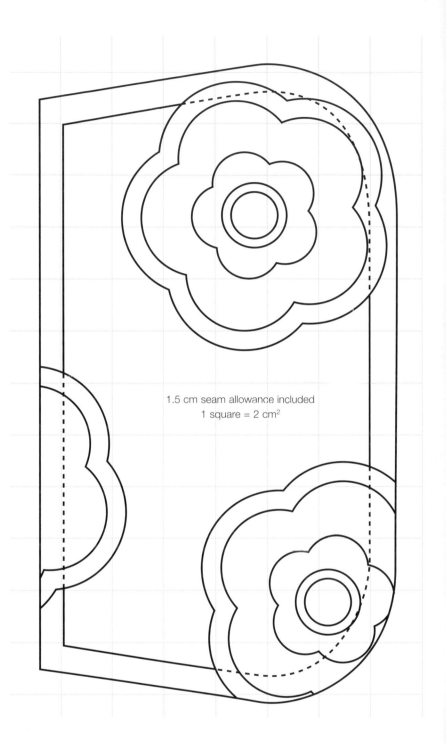

1.5 cm seam allowance included
1 square = 2 cm^2

Fold over the top edge of the bag and press flat. Repeat with the lining. Pin the ends of the handles to the inside of the bag at the side seams. Slip the lining into the bag,

WS together. Topstitch around the top edge of the bag, 1 cm from the edge. Remove the pins. Sew the press stud just inside the bag in the centre to close it.

Urban chic

TWEED-EFFECT HANDBAG
Size: 28 x 31 cm

MATERIALS
2 x 50 cm squares of reversible felt (one side light green, one side dark green) ● Scissors ● Thick tapestry wool: one skein each of light, medium and dark green ● Masking tape ● Matching sewing thread ● Pins ● 2 leather handles ● 2 rectangles 33 x 30 cm of cotton (for the lining).

METHOD
Cut a rectangle of felt 33 x 30 cm for each side of the bag. From remaining fabric, cut out 4 panels measuring 33 x 8 cm each. On one bag side, lay 2 dark green panels over the light green side, making sure they are spaced equidistant from outer edges. Repeat with other side. Topstitch panels to bag sides. Take 3 strands of tapestry wool of varying thicknesses and colours and tape strands together at one end. Plait them together to create a piece that is 35 cm in length. Make 11 of these in total.

Lay the plaited tapestry wool vertically between the panels, hold them in place with masking tape, then attach them using a zigzag stitch – varying the width of the stitch depending on the thickness of the plait. Carefully remove the masking tape as you go along. Repeat horizontally with the other strips, using the photo for placement reference. Trim ends to align with fabric edge.

With RS facing, sew the sides and bottom of the bag together 1 cm in from the edges.

Cut 8 rectangles of 8 x 2 cm from the scraps of felt. Pin them together, dark sides facing and sew them together along each side. Fold each one around a handle ring to create handle loops. With RS together, pin the loops to the inside edge of fabric, spacing them 8 cm apart, with the handles inside of the bag. Assemble the lining, leaving an opening of 10 cm in the seam of the bottom edge.

Slide the bag inside the lining, RS together. Stitch around the top of the bag, catching the bag handles into the seam as you go.

Turn the bag RS out. Hand sew the opening in the lining, then slip the lining into the bag. Topstitch around the top edge of the bag, 1 cm from the edge.

Urban chic

SUMMER SEQUINS
Size: 30 x 30 cm

MATERIALS
80 cm of heavy unbleached canvas ● 80 cm of heavy striped cotton (for the lining) ● Scissors ● Dressmaker's carbon ● Variety of sequins, beads, velvet flowers and clover leaves, and fabric leaves and rosebuds ● Pins ● Matching sewing thread ● Embroidery thread of various colours ● Green embroidery thread for the stems ● Embroidery needle.

STITCHES USED
Couching stitch (see page 125).

METHOD
Following the pattern on page 100, cut out the bag and handles in the canvas and the cotton, adding 1.5 cm for the side seams and 2.5 cm for the hem at the top of the bag. Enlarge the templates on page 101 and transfer the design onto what will be the front of the canvas bag using dressmaker's carbon. Enlarge the flower and leaf details on page 100 and transfer the design to both sides of the bag.

Lay all appliqué motifs onto the fabric and pin in place. Use a zigzag stitch to stitch around the motifs.

To work the beading, begin with a basic 'stop' bead at the end of the thread. Place a bead on the thread and then loop back through it to secure the end of the thread and prevent the beads from falling off. Using the diagram as a reference, sew the beads for each motif by threading enough beads to create your base row. Sew in place and insert the thread through the beads and into the fabric to secure. Continue with the next rows until the motif is complete. Repeat with each flower.

Using diagram as reference, apply sequins by overlapping or attaching them in rows (see page 100).

Attach the little rosebuds in place with a few invisible stitches. To make their stems, pin green embroidery thread in position and attach it with couching stitch. Remove pins.

To make up the bag, sew up the sides, RS together, 1.5 cm from the edges. Iron seams open. Fold over 2.5 cm around the top of the bag and iron flat. Make up the lining in the same way and slide it into the bag, WS facing.

Fold over 1.5 cm down both sides of each of the handle pieces and iron flat. Pin a canvas and a cotton handle piece together, WS facing, and stitch down both sides. Slip the ends of the handles in position between the bag and the lining and pin in place. Stitch around the top edge of the bag, removing the pins as you go along.

(see also pages 100–1)

Urban chic

ELEGANT STRIPES

MATERIALS

Ticking: enough to cover inside and outside of the cardboard folder, allowing 5 cm extra on all sides ● Scissors ● Thick cardboard, scored and folded in half widthways ● PVA or white paper glue ● Glue brush ● Ruler ● 4 metal grommets ● 4 small metal eyelets ● Grommet kit ● Hammer or mallet ● 3 m of leather laces.

METHOD

Cut a piece of fabric large enough to cover the outside of the folder, allowing an extra 5 cm all around. Cut another piece large enough to cover the inside, leaving a border of 2 cm on all sides.

Spread the glue evenly over the whole of the outside of the cardboard, then carefully lay the larger piece of fabric on top. Draw the edge of a ruler across the surface to ensure that the fabric sticks evenly to the cardboard and to remove any air bubbles. Fold over the fabric edges to the WS of the cardboard, pinching the corners and cutting them off right at the edges of the cardboard to prevent bulky corners.

Fold over 2 cm all around the remaining piece of fabric, iron flat, then glue it to the inside of the cardboard folder in the same manner as before.

Use the hole punch from the grommet kit to punch 2 holes on each fabric edge for the handles. Position the grommet on the tool and poke through one of the holes. Position the matching grommet piece over the first piece and use the hammer or mallet to join the 2 pieces. Repeat with the 3 other holes and the eyelets on the sides. Plait laces to form 2 handles, knotting the ends behind each eyelet. Thread the remaining 2 laces through the holes on each side. These can be knotted or tied in a bow to close the bag.

Urban chic

WINE BOTTLE BAG
Size: 32 x 22 cm

MATERIALS
2 rectangles 36 x 23 cm of heavy unbleached linen ● Mother-of-pearl buttons of various sizes ● Beige and blue heavy-duty thread ● Needle ● Pins ● String.

STITCHES USED
Couching stitch (see page 125).

METHOD
Sew the buttons in place on one of the linen rectangles to form a bunch of grapes. Pin a length of string above them to form the vine tendril and attach it to the fabric using couching stitch.

Pin the 2 linen rectangles together, RS facing, and sew them along the bottom and side edges, 1.5 cm in from the edge. Overstitch all seams. Fold over 5 mm around the top edge, then fold over again 2 cm and pin. Cut 2 equal lengths of string for the bag handles. Sew the top edge seam, catching the ends of the 2 lengths of string in the stitching to form the handles.

Urban chic

PUNCHED AND PLAITED LEATHER
Size: 35 x 26 cm

MATERIALS
Very sharp scissors (such as kitchen scissors) ● 100 x 50 cm piece of leather ● Ballpoint pen ● Cutting board ● 5 and 12 mm leather punch ● Size D (6 mm) oval punch ● Hammer or mallet ● Vinyl acetate glue or rubber cement ● 10 m of leather thong.

METHOD
Enlarge the pattern on pages 102–3 and cut out the pieces. Lay these templates on the WS of the leather and draw around the edges with a ballpoint pen.

On the RS of the leather, mark the positions of all the holes with the pen. They will need to be perfectly aligned so that you can assemble the bag correctly. Draw the arabesque pattern on the front.

Place the leather on the cutting board and punch out all the shapes using the leather punch. Form the oval shapes using the oval punch. Glue the lining to the gusset, WS together, with a line of glue along each edge and in the centre. Glue the top lining pieces in place with a line of glue along the lower edges. To make up the bag, lay a side panel and one side of the front together, WS facing, lining up the holes. Make a strong knot in 1 end of a leather thong, then, beginning at the top, join the 2 pieces by threading it through the holes as far as the middle of the gusset. Fold the bag so that the top of the back panel lines up with the other side of this side panel. Lace down this side to the bottom. Tie the 2 ends with a firm knot.

To make the handles, make 2 plaits about 75 cm long using 3 thongs each. Thread the ends of each plait from the inside to the outside at A, then back in again at B. Knot the ends inside the bag. If you have enough thongs left, knot some fringes at the bottom of the bag.

(see also pages 102–3)

Urban chic

RIBBON ROSES
Size: 36 x 30 cm

MATERIALS
50 cm of heavy linen ● Scissors ● Sewing and embroidery needles ● White sewing thread ● 82 cm strip of strong paper ● DMC Cordonnet special: 1 skein of ecru ● Tracing paper ● Pencil ● Dressmaker's carbon ● DMC stranded embroidery thread: 1 skein each of very light fern green 524, very light yellow green 772, medium raspberry 3832 and light raspberry 3833 ● Ribbon: 5 m x 25 mm-wide fuchsia, pink and dark purple; 5 m x 40 mm-wide pink; 5 m x 35 mm-wide ecru 367 and green 161 ● White seed beads ● Very fine needle ● 45 cm fine linen for the lining ● 30 x 10 cm of thin cardboard.

STITCHES USED
Knotted herringbone insertion stitch (see page 104); stem stitch, straight stitch and satin stitch (see page 125).

METHOD
Cut 1 rectangle of 82 x 33 cm (A), 1 of 82 x 7 cm (B) for the bag and 2 of 44 x 6 cm for the handles. Fold over 1 cm along the lengths of bag pieces A and B and iron flat. Tack folded edges next to each other onto strong paper, leaving a 5 mm gap between them. Using the Cordonnet thread, join them together with knotted herringbone insertion stitch. Remove tacking stitches and paper. Enlarge the design on page 105 and transfer it onto the front of the bag (centre of fabric) using dressmaker's carbon. Embroider the stems in stem stitch, the leaves in satin stitch and the buds in straight stitch. Work the leaves and buds around the roses in green and ecru ribbon.

Make the roses (see page 104), repeating steps 6–8 until each rose has reached the desired size (twist the ribbon to create a rose shape.) Sew the roses and beads in place. To assemble the bag, fold it RS facing, and sew up the side, 1 cm in from the edge. Iron open the seam. Fold the bag flat, placing this seam in the middle of the back. Sew the bottom edges together. Fold up the corners of this seam by 5 cm and sew along the fold. Cut off corners to make a 10 cm-wide gusset.

Make the lining for the lower part of the bag (A) in the same way as the bag itself. Place the card in the gusset and slip the lining into the bag, WS together. Hand stitch the lining to the bag just below the line of knotted herringbone insertion stitch. To make the handles, fold each strip lengthways, RS together. Sew along the edges. Turn the handles RS out and iron them flat with the seam in the middle of the underside. Pin handles, facing down, inside the top edge of each side of the bag, spacing the ends 14 cm apart.

Sew up the sides of the smaller piece of the lining (B) and sew the seams together. Pin into position outside the bag, RS facing, and machine stitch around the top, catching the ends of the handles into the seam as you sew.

Turn the bag RS out and sew the bottom of the top lining in place just above the insertion stitching.

(see also pages 104–5)

Urban chic

BEADED CANVAS

Sizes: 14 x 27 cm (small bag); 28 x 40 cm (large bag)

MATERIALS

1.2 m of double thread tapestry canvas in antique (wash well before use to distress the fabric) ● Scissors ● Needle ● Beige sewing thread ● Pins ● 300 5 mm-diameter matt gold beads ● DMC stranded embroidery thread in medium old gold 729 ● Water-erasable pen.

METHOD FOR SMALL BAG

Cut a 45 x 29 cm rectangle of canvas for the bag and 2 rectangles of 24 x 4 cm for the handles. Fold the large piece in 2 to obtain a rectangle of 29 x 22.5 cm. With RS together, tack along the fold (gusset) line.

Sew the sides together. To form the gusset, flatten the bag so that the side seam is on top of the tacking line. Stitch at 90° to this line 4.5 cm in from the corner. Cut off the point. Do the same on the other side of the bag to give a 9 cm-wide base. Turn the bag RS out.

Fold over the top of the bag by 5 mm, then 1.5 cm and press flat.

To make the handles, fold over 5 mm down both sides of each length, then fold them lengthways, WS facing. Sew them together along the edges.

Pin both ends of one handle inside the top of the bag, spacing them 9 cm apart and equidistant from each side. Repeat with the other handle on the other side. Machine stitch the hem at the top of the bag, fixing the handles in place and removing the pins as you go, then topstitch along the top edge.

Decorate the bag with 3 rows of beads: thread the beads (about 200) onto the gold embroidery thread. Pin to the bag, then, using the beige thread, fix in place with a small stitch over the gold thread between each bead. Thread the ends of the gold thread through the bag and knot on the other side.

METHOD FOR LARGE BAG

Cut a 70 x 42 cm rectangle of canvas for the bag and 2 rectangles of 30 x 5 cm for the handles. Fold the large piece in 2 to obtain a rectangle of 42 x 35 cm. Follow the instructions for making the small bag but stitching the gusset of the bag 5 cm from the corners to create a 10 cm-wide gusset.

Draw the monogram onto the front of the bag using a water-erasable pen, then fix the beads in place following the method given for the small bag.

Urban chic

FEMININE CHARM
Size : 28 x 38 cm

MATERIALS
50 cm of linen (for the bag) ●
50 cm of silk (for the lining) ●
Scissors ● Pins ● Assorted pieces
of recycled lace, embroidery,
ribbon, etc. ● Sewing thread.

METHOD
Cut out the pattern pieces, allowing an extra 2 cm along the top edge of the front and back of the bag and a 1 cm seam allowance around all other sides.

Pin the various recycled pieces of lace, embroidery and ribbon onto the linen front piece. Machine or hand stitch them in place.

Make up the lining and the linen bag in the same way: sew 2 darts at the top of front and back pieces to reduce the top length to 30 cm. Join the gusset to the front piece, RS together, 8 mm from the edges, then sew the strip to the back piece. Fold over 2 cm around the top of the bag and iron flat.

Stitch the 2 handles together, RS facing, leaving the ends open. Turn the handle RS out.

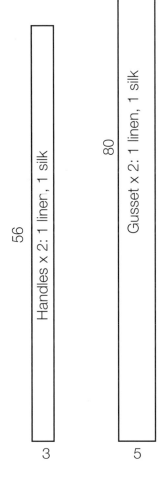

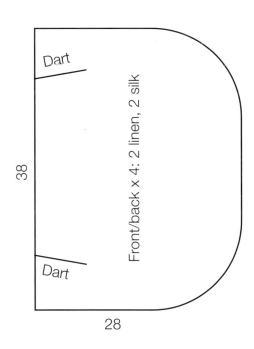

Slip the lining into the bag, WS facing, and pin around the top. Pin the ends of the handle between the 2 layers at either side of the bag, equidistant from the edge. Machine stitch around the top of the bag. Remove pins.

Urban chic

THE LILY AND THE BUTTERFLY
Size: 40 x 35 cm

MATERIALS
90 x 39 cm of heavy, dark brown canvas ● Dark brown sewing thread ● White fabric-marking pencil ● Orange, purple and pink fabric paints ● Bronze and orange seed beads ● 2.5 m of 25 mm-wide claret-coloured webbing.

METHOD
Oversew all the edges of the fabric. Fold the bag in half widthways, WS facing. Iron flat and unfold. Using the fabric-marking pencil, trace over the fold line. Mark a parallel line 5 cm on either side of the centre line. This will eventually be the gusset. Enlarge the design on page 106 and trace over it. Go over it on the WS using the fabric-marking pencil. Place the design on the lower right corner of one side of the canvas. Trace over all the lines in pencil to transfer the white pencil design onto the fabric.

Paint over the design using the photo for inspiration and following the manufacturer's instructions. When the paint is dry, decorate the flower by sewing on the seed beads. Draw parallel lines 11 cm from each edge of the fabric. Pin the webbing along these lines from the centre of fabric piece to the edge, upwards, to create a 38 cm handle, and return to the centre. Continue the webbing to the other side and repeat, returning back to centre. Sew along each edge of the webbing, stopping 3 cm from the top edge of the bag. Sew 1 cm in around the top edges.

Fold the bag in half, RS together, and sew up the sides, 1 cm in from the edges.

Fold the bottom of the bag as shown in the diagram on page 106, and sew a 10 cm seam at 90° to the side seam to form the gusset of the bag. Fold the top edges of the bag over 3 cm and iron flat. Topstitch around the top edge of the bag.

(see also pages 106–7)

Out and about

FULL OF NOSTALGIA
Size: 32 x 30 cm

MATERIALS
60 cm of striped fabric ● Scissors ● Sewing thread of contrasting colours ● Sewing machine with decorative stitches ● Pins ● 50 cm of rickrack ● Embroidered or crocheted motifs.

METHOD
Cut out the pattern pieces, adding a 1.5 cm seam allowances around each piece. Cut 2 rectangles of 48 x 6 cm (straps) and 4 rectangles of 30 x 3 cm (ties).

Overstitch the edges of the front and back pieces. Using a decorative stitch, sew around the bottom and sides, 3 cm in from the edges.

Lay the bag pieces together, WS facing, and stitch 1.5 cm in from the edges, around the bottom and sides, stopping 7 cm from the top of each side. Iron open the seams. Hem the top of the sides using decorative stitching. Pin a few flat pleats at the top to reduce the width to 25 cm.

Lay the 2 edging pieces on top of each other, WS facing, and sew together the top and sides, 1.5 cm in from the edges. Fold the bottom edges over 1.5 cm onto the WS and iron flat. Repeat with the other 2 edging pieces. Turn RS out.

Slip the top 1.5 cm of the bag between the 2 edging layers on either side. Pin in place, then stitch all around the edges to join the 2 together, using different coloured threads and decorative stitches. Remove the pins as you go along. Sew a length of rickrack along the top edge of the bag.

For the shoulder straps, fold over both sides of each strip so that they meet in the middle, then sew down the middle using a zigzag stitch to overlap the 2 edges. Repeat with the side ties.

Sew a shoulder strap to each side of the bag, spacing the ends 8 cm apart and equidistant from the edges. Sew a tie to each side of the bag, halfway up the side openings. Knot the loose ends. Using decorative stitching, sew the motifs onto the bag front and back.

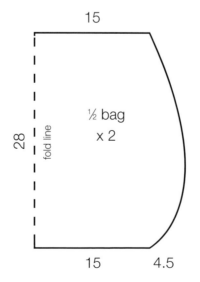

½ bag
x 2

15

28

fold line

15   4.5

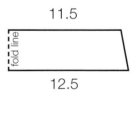

11.5

fold line

12.5

½ edging x 4

Out and about

WESTERN STYLE
Size: 36 x 34 cm

MATERIALS
**70 cm of brown suedette ●
Scissors ● Pins ● Brown thread.**

METHOD
Cut 2 rectangles of 60 x 34 cm and 2 straps of 95 x 3 cm from the fabric. Fold over a 12 cm flap at the top of each rectangle. Stitch 2 cm in from the fold. Slip a suedette strap through each.

Place the 2 rectangles together, with the folds on the outside, and pin in place. Stitch across the bag, 12 cm up from the bottom edge, then again 2 cm above that.

Slip the ends of both straps between these 2 rows of stitching on each side and pin in place.

Stitch up the sides of the bag, 2 cm in from the edges, beginning 2 cm from the top and stopping at the lower row of stitching at the `bottom, fixing the straps in place in the seam at the bottom. Do not catch top folds in the seam. Remove pins.

Cut the folds at the top, and the bottom 12 cm of the bag, into fringes 10 cm long and 1 cm wide.

Out and about

ARTIST'S SATCHEL
Size: 18 x 25 cm

MATERIALS
60 cm of floral fabric ● 1.2 m x 30 cm of checked fabric ● 1 m x 60 cm of striped fabric ● Scissors ● 2 rectangles 25 x 9 cm of thick iron-on interfacing (plus medium-weight if chosen fabrics are very fine) ● White heavy-duty thread ● 50 cm of 6 mm-wide woven elastic ● 5 buttons ● 1 m x 5 cm medium-thick cotton fleece ● Thin cardboard or plastic.

METHOD
The bag is composed of 2 parts: an outer part – bag C (the whole of the template) + sides G and H – and an inner part of the same area but divided into segments – D, E, F, K, I and J – to enable card or plastic pieces to be inserted between the 2 layers to stiffen the whole. (These can be removed before the bag is washed.) There are also 2 pockets sewn onto the outside.

Cut out the pattern pieces on pages 108–9, adding a 1 cm seam allowance around each piece. Cut pieces C, G and H in the floral fabric and D, E, F, I, J and K in the striped fabric, ensuring stripes run in the same direction on the pieces.

To make the sides of the bag, iron the interfacing onto the back of pieces G and H. Sew G to I, RS facing, leaving a small opening. Turn RS out, iron, then sew up the opening. Repeat with H and J.

To make the side pocket, cut out B in the checked fabric. Fold edge over twice, iron and sew a double hem 1 cm across the top. Pin 2 darts along the bottom edge to reduce its width to 9 cm. Stitch the base to secure the darts. Fold over 1 cm along the bottom and side edges and iron flat. Sew the pocket to G or H.

To make the big pocket, cut 2 A pieces in the floral fabric. Fix 2 elastic loops in the seam (see template). Sew pieces together, RS facing, 1 cm from the edges, leaving an opening at the bottom. Turn the pocket RS out and iron flat. Sew up the opening by hand. Cut 2 15 cm lengths of checked

fabric and sew them onto the pocket, parallel to each other and 15 cm apart, to form little loops.

To make the small pocket, cut 2 A^1 pieces and 2 rectangles of 10 x 8 cm in the checked fabric. Sew the 2 A^1 pieces together, WS together, leaving an opening in the seam. Turn RS out, iron flat and sew up the opening. Do the same with the 2 rectangles. Sew the rectangle onto the bottom of A^1, 1 cm from the edges, leaving the top open. Turn RS out. Add a button loop to the point of A^1. Fold over the point onto the pocket and sew a button in place opposite the button loop. Sew the pocket onto A (on the same side as brush loops, see template).

Lay the central part of A onto the RS of C, superimposing on line de. Sew together along the sides and across the bottom (line de on piece A). Fold up the bottom of A and fold over the flap at the top. Sew 2 buttons opposite the elastic loops to close the pocket.

(continues on page 108)

Out and about

CHESTNUT SEASON
Size: 35 x 40 cm

MATERIALS
35 cm each of brown woollen fabric, printed cotton and iron-on interfacing ● Scissors ● White dressmaker's carbon ● Embroidery hoop and needle ● DMC stranded embroidery thread: 1 skein of each of greens: 165, 166, 733, 3819; browns: 300, 801, 938, 3371; beiges: 612, 613, 822, 3822, 3823; oranges: 728, 783 ● Sewing thread ● 2 buttons.

STITCHES USED
Using 2 strands of embroidery thread: satin stitch, encroaching satin stitch and straight stitch (see page 125).

METHOD
Cut 2 rectangles of 25 x 40 in the woollen fabric, printed cotton and interfacing (adding a 1.5 cm seam allowance around all sides in the wool and cotton). Cut 1 strip of 75 x 6 cm in both fabrics and in the interfacing for the shoulder straps. Enlarge the template on page 110 and, using dressmaker's carbon, transfer it onto the lower part of RS of one of the woollen pieces.

Place the fabric into the embroidery hoop and embroider the design using the colours and stitches shown on the template. Iron the back using a damp cloth, with a soft cloth placed underneath the embroidered surface to protect it. Iron the interfacing onto all the woollen pieces.

Make up the bag by sewing the front and back of the bag together, WS facing, around the sides and bottom. Do the same with the printed fabric lining, leaving an opening in the bottom.

Slide the bag inside the lining, RS together. Sew around the top edge. Turn the bag RS out and close the seam in the lining. Slip the lining into the bag.

Sew the 2 strap pieces together, WS facing, leaving an opening in one side. Turn the strap RS out and close the opening. Pin each side of the strap to the side of the bag. Sew the ends of the strap with a square of stitching, then an 'X' through the centre for added strength. Sew buttons over the top of them.

(see also page 110)

Out and about

NATURAL KNAPSACK
Size: 40 cm tall, 38 cm in diameter

MATERIALS
Heavy burlap: 2 rectangles of 92 x 50 cm and 2 circles of 32 cm-diameter ● Scissors ● Heavy-duty sewing thread ● 1.5 m of 8 cm-wide upholstery webbing, cut into 2 equal lengths ● Pins ● 8 grommets ● Grommet kit ● Hammer or mallet ● String.

METHOD
Make each of the rectangles into a tube by sewing the 2 shorter (50 cm) lengths together, RS facing, 2 cm in from the edges. Leave an opening of 15 cm in one of the tubes (the lining).

Pin one end of each of the webbing straps to the bottom edge of the outer bag, spacing them 13 cm on either side of the vertical seam. Stitch the strap to the bag, 1 cm in from the edges. Sew each tube around one of the circles, stitching 2 cm in from the edges.

Pin the other ends of the webbing straps at the top of the bag, placing them 6 cm away from the vertical seam on either side of the bag.

Slip the bag inside the lining, WS facing, and stitch together around the top, 8 cm in from the edges. Turn the bag RS out through the opening in the lining. Hand stitch the opening closed. Topstitch around the top edge of the bag.

Use the hole punch from the grommet kit to punch 8 holes around the top of the bag, spacing them about 10 cm apart. Position the grommet on the tool and poke through one of the holes. Position the matching grommet piece over the first piece and use the hammer or mallet to join the 2 pieces. Repeat with the others.

Thread the string through the grommets to close the bag. If you wish, you can decorate the ends with wooden leaf shapes. Make a hole in the top of each shape and glue the end of the string inside.

Out and about

HIDDEN BEAUTY

MATERIALS
1 khaki holdall ● Printed cotton fabric (meterage as per the bag, see method) ● Scissors ● Khaki and white heavy-duty sewing thread ● Fabric glue ● 2-tone ribbon (see method).

METHOD
To make the cotton lining, take the dimensions of the front and back of the bag (2 rectangles with rounded corners) and gusset (top + sides + bottom). Cut each piece in the cotton fabric, adding a 2 cm seam allowance all the way around. Stitch the band to the front and back pieces, WS together.

Slit open a strip the length of the zip along the middle of the top edge. Fold over and sew a small hem on each side of this opening. Slip the lining into the holdall, WS facing, and glue the lining seams to those of the bag. Machine stitch each side of bag along the edge of the zip teeth.

Glue the ribbon along the middle of the webbing handles and on the pocket flap, if there is one.

Out and about

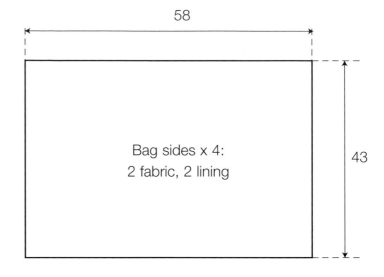

Bag sides x 4:
2 fabric, 2 lining

58

43

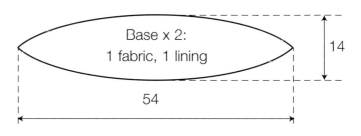

Base x 2:
1 fabric, 1 lining

54

14

WORLD TRAVELLER
Size: 40 x 56 cm

MATERIALS

50 cm of khaki canvas ● 1 m of Chinese-print fabric ● Scissors ● Oriental food packaging, holiday photos, postcards, maps, drilled coins ● 20 x 20 cm of clear plastic sheeting ● Sewing thread of various colours ● Glue ● Khaki and red embroidery thread ● Embroidery needle ● Pencil ● 2 leather handles.

METHOD

Cut out the pattern pieces in the Chinese-print fabric and canvas, as shown, adding 1 cm to the shorter length (the height of the bag) in the lining fabric.

Position the flattened packaging, photos, postcards, maps, etc. onto a khaki rectangle, leaving the centre area clear for the compass. Cut rectangles of clear plastic sheeting slightly larger than the chosen objects and place them over the top. Machine stitch along the edges of the plastic using a very close zigzag stitch. Trim the edges of the plastic right to the stitching.

Cut the compass shape and the outer rim from a map and glue them in the centre of the bag front. Sew a drilled coin between each of the points of the compass.

Lay a circle of clear plastic over the top and sew in place as before, adding a few stitches in the centre. Embroider the cardinal points of the compass around the circle.

Use a pencil to 'caption' the various documents and to draw a 'route' line, with directional arrows to join them up. Embroider these lines and words in backstitch using coloured sewing thread. Add a drilled coin at the top in the centre. Make up the exterior and lining of

the bag, separately, in the same way: with WS facing, sew the sides of the front and back pieces together, 1 cm from the edge. Iron open the seams. Sew the base to the front and back. Fold over 2 cm all around the top of the bag and iron flat.

Cut a 40 x 6 cm rectangle of fabric. With RS facing, sew the side together, 1 cm away from the edge. Turn RS out and cut into 4 equal lengths. Thread each through the ring of a leather handle and firmly sew the ends together.

Slip the lining into the bag (it will show at the top) and pin the handles between the 2 layers on each side. Topstitch around the top edge.

Out and about

A COLLECTION OF WASH BAGS

Materials and methods are given below for each bag in the photograph, from bottom to top

DOLLY BAG
Size: 20 x 20 cm

MATERIALS
50 cm of floral fabric ● Scissors ● Pins ● Sewing thread ● Safety pin.

METHOD
Cut 4 squares of 23 x 23 cm in the floral fabric. Round off 2 of the corners of each piece to shape at the base of the bag.

To make the lining, sew 2 squares together, with RS facing, along the bottom and sides, stitching 1.5 cm from the edges.

Cut 2 fabric strips of 8 x 1 cm. Make a small fold down each length and iron flat. Fold each strip lengthways, WS together, and topstitch down each side. Fold the strips in half to make loops. Sew together, 1 cm from edge.

To make the exterior of the bag, place the remaining 2 squares RS together. Pin a loop to each side, 2 cm from the top on each side. Sew up the sides and base, leaving an opening between 3 and 4 cm at the top of each side. Turn RS out and iron flat.

Slip the lining into the bag (WS facing) and sew around the top 4 cm in from the edge, then again 3 cm lower. Fold the top of each layer over 1 cm onto the WS. Sew together just in from the edge.

Cut 2 fabric strips of 60 x 2 cm for the ties. Make them following the instructions above for the loops. Thread them through each drawstring pocket, pull tight and knot the ends. To open the bag, pull on the loops.

SHAVING KIT
Size: 20 x 30 cm

MATERIALS
70 cm of animal-print fabric ● Scissors ● Pins ● Sewing thread ● 70 cm-long zip.

METHOD
Using template A on page 111, cut out 2 pieces, extending the back by 10 cm so back dimensions are 30 x 30 cm. (The additional length will become a side panel.) Add a 1 cm seam allowance to all edges. With RS together, sew the back to each end, starting from the corner of adjacent sides. Snip the corners of each side and diagonally on the front corners (to make folding easier). Fold side and front edges 1 cm inwards, then iron. Make up the lining in the same way.

Tack one tape of the zip under the edge of the top piece and the other around the bag edge. Insert the lining into the bag, WS facing. Sew around the bag edge and top piece, stitching through all 3 layers: the bag, the zip and the lining.

SPONGE BAG
Size: 20 x 30 cm

MATERIALS
60 cm of printed fabric ● 60 cm of co-ordinating fabric (for the lining) ● Scissors ● Sewing thread ● Pins ● 30 cm-long zip.

(continues on page 111)

For children

FOR DOLLY'S CLOTHES
Size: 40 x 32 cm

MATERIALS
84 x 42 cm of ivory linen (12 threads per cm) ● Scissors ● Sewing thread ● DMC stranded embroidery thread: 1 skein each of 471, 472, 680, 744, 924, 928, 945, 3064, 3688, 3777, 3809, white ● Tapestry, embroidery and sewing needles ● 1.5 m of 23 mm-wide ribbon ● Safety pin.

METHOD
Fold over 1 cm along each 84 cm length and 5 mm then 1.5 cm along each 42 cm edge. For the drawstring channel, overstitch the top hems, 1.5 cm in from edge. Overstitch the lengths.

Fold the fabric in half, RS together, and iron to mark the bottom fold. Mark the vertical centre of the front of the bag, then, following the template on pages 112–13, cross-stitch the design, using 3 strands of embroidery thread. Iron on the back using a damp cloth, with a soft cloth placed underneath the embroidered surface to protect it. Fold the bag RS together and sew up the sides, stopping just below the top hem on either side.

Attach a safety pin to one end of the ribbon to slide it through the top seam of the bag.

(see also pages 112–3)

For children

WINNING GOLDFISH
Size: 27 x 27 cm

MATERIALS
**84 x 30 cm of white linen ●
Scissors ● Pins ● White sewing
thread ● 30 ml plastic pipette ●
Clear gutta ● Pale blue fabric dye
and fixing agent ● Salt ● Large
bowl ● Pencil ● Sheet of clear
plastic ● Scalpel ● 20 x 10 cm
heavy white cotton ● Red, black
and iridescent silver-white fabric
paints ● Paintbrush or stencil
brush ● Red embroidery thread
and ● Needle.**

METHOD
Fold over and stitch a double hem
5 mm all around the linen rectangle.
Fold each end 27 cm into the
middle. Iron to mark the folds, then
open up. Following the diagrams
on page 114, fold along the dotted
lines: first take A onto J, overlapping
it by 5 mm, then fold B onto J.
(These 2 folds should overlap by
5 mm.) Turn over the fabric with the
unfolded piece at the top and fold
over edge D to meet C. (Edge E will
overlap the other fold by 5 mm.)
Sew together A/B and E/F. Turn the
bag RS out. Topstitch the seams.
Wash the bag and leave to dry.
Using the pipette and the gutta,
draw a 1 cm-wide line halfway
down and all the way around the
bag, on the inside and on the
outside. Leave to dry. Dissolve a
pinch of blue fabric dye, half a
sachet of fixing agent and a pinch of
salt in 5 litres of hot water and mix
well. Suspend the bag in the dye
as far as the line of gutta and leave
for 10 minutes. Rinse the bag in
cold water until the water runs clear.
Draw the outlines of the 3 goldfish
on the sheet of plastic freehand.
(Alternatively, enlarge the template
on page 114 and transfer it to the
plastic.) Using the scalpel, cut out
the fish shapes, then cut out the
scale details of each fish piece.
Place the hollowed stencil on the
front of the white cotton fabric and,
using the stencil brush or
paintbrush and red fabric paint,
paint the goldfish. Leave to dry, then
using the other template, add the
scale details in iridescent silver-white
and the eyes in black.

Leave to dry completely, then iron
the fabric on the front and back to
fix the paints.
Cut out the 3 goldfish and sew
them onto the centre of the bag
with red embroidery thread, using
overlapping long and short blanket
stitch all around the edges.

(see also page 114)

For children

TEDDY PORTRAIT
Size: 23 x 20 cm

MATERIALS
Dark brown felt: 2 rectangles 23 x 20 cm (for the front and back of the bag), 2 rectangles 32 x 4 cm (for the handles), and 3 x 2 cm (for the nose) ● 20 x 18 cm of light blue fleece fabric (for the bear) ● 8 x 8 cm dark blue woollen fabric (for the muzzle) ● 5 x 1.5 cm of red fleece fabric (for the badge) ● 2 small circles of white fleece fabric (for the eyes) ● Scissors ● Pins ● Light blue and dark brown sewing thread.

METHOD
Enlarge the pattern pieces on page 115 and cut out the various pieces in the fabrics. Pin the eyes, muzzle and nose onto the bear's face and sew them in place using light blue thread and a zigzag stitch along the edges of each piece. Form the mouth in brown zigzag stitches and the pupils with a few brown straight stitches. Sew the badge on the bear's chest.

Pin the bear onto the RS of a bag rectangle, lining up the pieces at the bottom edge. Attach the bear using brown zigzag stitches all around the edges. Stitch the ears, neck and arms in the same way.

Fold the handle pieces WS together and sew along their lengths with blue zigzag stitches, leaving 3 cm at each end. Open the ends of each handle. Pin a handle to the WS of the front, spacing the ends 8 cm apart. Repeat with the other handle on the back.

Sew across the top edge of the bag with a light blue zigzag stitch, catching the handles into the seam. Lay the 2 sides of the bag WS together and sew around the edges with a zigzag stitch, using blue thread against the brown bag edges and brown over the bear's chest at the bottom of the bag.

(see also page 115)

For children

CROCHETED RABBIT
Size: 15 x 20 cm

MATERIALS
Linen crochet thread: 70 g x terracotta, 70 g x pale green ● 3 mm crochet hook ● 4 x 14 mm-diameter wooden beads ● 20 x 10 cm strip of cardboard ● Fabric glue ● 2 x 20 cm lengths of wire.

STITCHES USED
Double crochet: on a base chain.
Stitch pattern at base: half trebles.
Edging: * work one double crochet, 3 half trebles and one double into 1 st, miss 2 st. * Cont from * to end.

TENSION
One square of 10 cm in double crochet using a no. 3 crochet hook = 24 st and 25 rows.

METHOD
For the base, make 45 chains in pale green. Work 10 cm in half trebles (working a turning chain at each end of the row). Fasten off.
Take the terracotta thread and crochet 144 double crochet around the edge of the base: (47 st along each length, 25 st along each

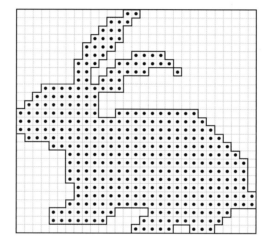

☐ Terracotta
● Pale green

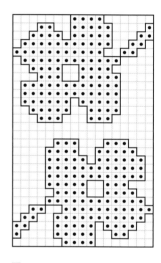

☐ Terracotta
● Pale green

width). Work 4 rounds of double crochet, then change to half trebles. Begin the rabbit on the 15th of 47 st along the lengths, the flower on the 12th of 25 st along the widths. Continue in terracotta until the work measures 13.5 cm in height, then crochet 1 row of double crochet in pale green, then 1 row of edging, then fasten off.
Sew the cardboard into the bottom of the bag. Thread the beads onto some pale green thread and then

sew them at the bottom corners of the bag.
Cover the wire lengths by working double crochet around them in pale green. Curve them and sew them onto the inside edge of each bag to form the handles.

à la
basse-
cour

For children

LADYBIRD STORY
Size: 30 x 28 cm

MATERIALS
2 rectangles of fine white linen, each 33 x 30 cm ● Tracing paper ● Dressmaker's carbon ● DMC stranded embroidery thread: 1 skein each of red, black, light green and dark green ● Embroidery needle ● Black iron-on fabric ● Double-sided iron-on interfacing ● Scissors ● 30 cm of red gingham ● Fabric glue ● Black felt ● Black fabric pen ● Pins.

STITCHES USED
Running stitch and satin stitch (see page 125).

METHOD
Enlarge the text on page 116 and transfer it onto the front of one of the linen rectangles using dressmaker's carbon. (Alternatively, use any familiar rhyme written out in a decorative script.) Embroider it in small running stitches using 2 strands of red embroidery thread. Transfer the shapes for the ladybirds' bodies onto the black iron-on fabric, and the wings onto iron-on interfacing. Cut out the wings, then iron the other side of the interfacing onto a small piece of gingham. Cut around all shapes. Using fabric glue, stick the bodies in place on the linen, then the wings. Use a running stitch and black embroidery thread to embroider the line and the ladybirds' feet and antennae. Mark the spots with the black fabric pen. Transfer the clover-leaf design to the fabric and embroider it using satin stitch and 2 shades of green embroidery thread. Overstitch around the edge of each linen rectangle, then with RS facing, sew the sides and bottom together, 1 cm in from the edges.

To make the border for the top of the bag, cut a 58 x 10 cm strip from the gingham. With RS facing, sew the short ends together, 1 cm in from the edge. Fold in half lengthways, WS together, and iron flat. Fold in edges and iron. Pin in place around the top of the bag so that it slightly overlaps both sides of the top edge, then topstitch, folding over the ends.

To make the handles, cut 2 strips of gingham of 24 x 10 cm. Fold each strip, RS facing, and stitch the length, 1 cm in from the edge. Turn RS out. Topstitch down both sides of each one. Fold over the ends and pin to the inside of the bag, one handle on either side, 7 cm in from the side seams. Stitch in place.

(see also page 116)

For children

MY FAVOURITE PET

MATERIALS
Soft gel gloss ● Black and white photocopy of your chosen photograph (including border) ● Soft paintbrush ● Sponge ● Scissors ● White canvas bag (buy one or make the one on the previous spread) ● Pencil ● Rolling pin.

METHOD
Using a paintbrush, coat the image with soft gel gloss, being careful that it doesn't run over the edges. Place the coated side in position onto the fabric and burnish it by rolling the rolling pin over the back, pressing down hard, for at least 1 minute. Leave it to dry for 3 hours. To remove the paper, soak a sponge in warm water, wring it out well, then rub it very gently on the paper. The little rolls of paper that will form will be easy to remove, while the printed image will remain stuck to the fabric.

For children

CINDERELLA'S COACH
Size: 46 cm tall, 32 cm in diameter

MATERIALS
2 m of thick pink cotton fabric ● Scissors ● 50 cm of fleece ● 25 cm of green cotton fabric ● Pins ● Pink and green sewing thread ● 2 pink 50 cm-long zips ● Safety pin ● 25 cm of thin wire ● Small amount of wadding.

METHOD
Enlarge the pattern pieces on page 117 and cut out. Pin the segments onto the pink fabric. Cut out 20, leaving a seam allowance of 5 mm around each one. Cut out 10 segments in the fleece. Cut 2 stalks, 2 tendrils, 2 leaves and 1 stem base from the green fabric.

To make the exterior of the coach, pin 10 fleece segments to the WS of 10 pink ones (which will form the exterior of the bag). Assemble these lined segments by stitching them together, RS facing. Sew together 7 to make the body of the coach and a further 3 to make the door. Repeat with non-lined segments. Iron open the seams. Sew the 2 bands of 7 segments each together,

WS facing. Fold the edges between the 2 layers. Repeat with the exterior and the interior faces of the door. Fold edges between the 2 layers. Pin the fabric tapes of the zips between the 2 so as to form a circle, placing the pullers at the top. Machine stitch or hand sew them in place.

Cut a 6 cm-diameter circle from the green fabric. Fold over the edges and iron flat, then sew it onto the bottom of the pumpkin to hide the join of the 10 segments.

Sew a tendril onto each of the stalks (see template for position). Sew the 2 halves together, RS facing, leaving the top and bottom of the stalk and the ends of the tendrils open. Cut a 2 cm-diameter circle from the green fabric, allowing for a small seam allowance. Sew it around the top of the stalk. Attach a safety pin and turn the stem and stalk RS out.

Fold over the edges of the leaves onto the WS and iron flat. Pin them on top of each other WS together and slip the end of the tendril

between the 2 layers. Sew together around the edges. Machine stitch the veins on the leaves.

Fold over the edges of the stem base onto the WS and iron flat. Pin it onto the top of the pumpkin, slitting it over the top of the zips. Oversew it in place, tucking under the edges next to the zips.

Stuff the stalk with the wadding, then sew it onto to the top of the stem base. Insert wire into the tendrils and curl by wrapping the tendrils around your finger.

(see also page 117)

Shopping bags

SPRING COLLECTION

Sizes: 24 x 32 cm (shoulder and shopping bag), 32 x 20 cm (bucket bag)

STITCHES USED

Running stitch (see page 125) and French knots.

SHOULDER BAG

MATERIALS

Tobacco-coloured hessian: 2 rectangles 66 x 28 cm (for the bag and lining) and 2 strips 98 x 5 cm (for the strap) ● Dressmaker's chalk ● White tapestry wool ● Tapestry needle ● Scissors ● Pins ● Sewing thread ● Safety pin.

METHOD

Fold over 1 cm around each rectangle and iron flat. Fold one of the rectangles in half WS together. Using dressmaker's chalk, draw freehand or trace the outlines of 3 leaves across the middle of one half. Embroider in running stitch using the tapestry wool. Fold each rectangle widthways, RS together. Fold over 1 cm at the top of each bag onto the WS and iron flat. Pin, then stitch up the sides with RS together.
Slip the lining into the bag, WS together. Pin the 2 shoulder strap pieces RS together and stitch along their lengths. Attach a safety pin to one end to turn RS out, then iron. Slip the ends of the straps between the 2 top layers of the bag at the side seams and pin in place. Sew around the top edge of the bag, catching straps into the seam.

SHOPPING BAG

MATERIALS

Tobacco-coloured hessian: 2 rectangles 66 x 28 cm (for the bag and lining) and 2 strips 50 x 5 cm (for the straps) ● Dressmaker's chalk ● White tapestry wool ● Tapestry needle ● Scissors ● Pins ● Sewing thread ● Safety pin.

METHOD

Fold over 1 cm around each rectangle and iron flat. Draw a leaves and stem motif across the front and back in running stitch, using the tapestry wool.
Make up in the same way as the shoulder bag. Sew up the handle, then cut in half to create 2 straps and attach to both sides of the bag.

BUCKET BAG

MATERIALS

Tobacco-coloured hessian: 2 rectangles 82 x 38 cm (for the bag and lining) and 2 strips 40 x 5 cm (for the straps) ● Pins ● Sewing thread ● Scissors ● Dressmaker's chalk ● White tapestry wool ● Tapestry needle ● Safety pin.

METHOD

Fold over 1 cm around each rectangle and iron flat. Fold one of the rectangles in half widthways and iron flat. Stitch up the sides. Fold the bag to bring the bottom of the side seam onto the base fold. Stitch at 90° to this line 10 cm in from the corner to create a gusset. Cut off the point 1 cm from the seam. Do the same on the other side. Make up the lining bag in the same way. Draw a leaf design around the bag and, using tapestry wool, embroider in running stitch and French knots. Make up in the same way as the shoulder bag. Sew up the handle, then cut in half to create 2 straps and attach to both sides of the bag.

Shopping bags

A TRUE TOTE BAG
Sizes: 26 x 30 cm (bag); 14 x 22 cm (purse)

MATERIALS
100 g of DMC Cebelia 10 crochet cotton in ecru ● 1.25 mm crochet hook ● 2 small coils of mixed raffia ● Scissors ● 50 cm of unbleached linen ● Pins ● Thread ● 50 cm of striped canvas ● 30 cm of iron-on interfacing ● White cardboard ● Strands of thick cotton (for stuffing handles).

STITCHES USED
Chain stitch; double crochet; treble crochet; 4 treble crochets joined together: work 4 trebles, yarn round hook, slip through all loops on hook (1 loop remains on hook).

METHOD FOR THE BAG
Make 160 chain + 1 turning ch. Crochet following the pattern on page 118.

At each even row, take a raffia strand into the double crochets, taking care to ensure it stays flexible. Trim the raffia to 3 cm at the ends of the row. Continue for 62 cm. Iron with a damp cloth on the WS.

To line the bag, cut a piece of linen to the size of the crochet panel plus 1 cm at top and bottom. Fold over this 1 cm at the top and bottom edges onto the WS and iron flat. Pin the fabric and crochet panel WS together and stitch along the short edge. Trim the raffia.

For the side panels of the bag, cut 2 rectangles of striped canvas, each 28 x 11 cm. Apply iron-on interfacing to the WS. With RS facing, sew the crochet panel to the sides, 5 mm from the edges, matching centres. Slip a piece of white cardboard into the bottom of the bag between the crochet and the lining to make the base. Fold the excess at the top of the side panels to the inside and slip stitch down.

To line the side panels, cut 2 linen rectangles, adding a 1 cm seam allowance on all sides. Fold over 1 cm onto the WS on all sides, iron flat and hand sew to the inside of the bag. Sew the lining to the crochet panel at the top of the bag. To make the handles, cut rectangles of striped fabric on the bias, each 26 x 30 cm. Apply iron-on interfacing to the WS. Fold RS together lengthways and sew 5 mm from the edges. Turn RS out. Stuff with strands of thick cotton. Sew to the insides of the bag on each side.

METHOD FOR THE PURSE
Make 112 chain + 1 turning ch. Follow the pattern on page 118 for 33 cm. Iron with a damp cloth on the WS.

Cut a rectangle of linen the same size as the crochet panel, adding a 1 cm seam allowance all around. Iron the top and bottom edge to the WS and iron flat. Fold over a 5 mm double hem to the RS along the side edges and iron flat. Trim the raffia. Place the crochet on the fabric, sliding the crochet edges underneath the folded edges of the linen. Sew with small stitches along the 4 edges of the fabric.

Fold the bottom edge 13 cm over, WS together. Sew the sides. Fold the top down 6 cm to make the flap.

(see also page 118)

Shopping bags

TARTAN TOTE
Size: 48 x 30 cm

MATERIALS
77 x 50 cm of tartan woollen fabric ● Sewing and basting thread ● Scissors ● 2.8 m of webbing ● 77 x 50 cm lining fabric (or quilted plastic) ● 2 rectangles 50 x 27 cm of chintz (for the drawstring collar, optional) ● 2 m of cord ● 4 gold beads ● Safety pin.

METHOD
Fold the tartan in half, RS together, to form a 50 x 38.5 cm rectangle. Mark the fold with basting stitches. Sew the sides 1 cm from the edges. Iron open the seams.

Flatten the bag and fold up a corner so that the side seam lies against the line of basting. Sew at a 90° angle to the basting line, 6.5 cm from the corner. Trim the corner to 1 cm from the stitching. Repeat on the other side. Do the same with the lining.

Cut the webbing into 2 equal lengths and mark the midpoint of each. Pin both ends to one side of the basting line, 7 cm in from each end, then pin vertically up the sides of the bag. (The loop at the top will form the handle.) Repeat on the other side of the bag with the other length of webbing. Stitch each webbing strap to the bag along both edges, stopping 3 cm from the top of the bag.

Make up the lining in the same way as the bag. Slide the lining into the bag, WS together. Fold over the top edges of lining and fabric. Sew them 5 mm from the top, leaving the straps free.

To make the drawstring collar (optional), sew the 2 pieces of chintz, RS together, along the 27 cm edges, leaving a small opening in each seam 5 cm from the top. Fold over 1 cm, then another 3 cm at the top and iron flat. Slip the collar inside the bag, RS together, aligning the bottom edge to the top of the bag. Sew 1 cm from the edge. Fold the collar towards the inside and oversew 1 cm from the edge. Cut the cord in half and slide each piece into the drawstring channel created. Thread a bead onto each end before tying them together.

Shopping bags

KITCHEN GARDEN
Size: 40 x 35 cm

MATERIALS

50 cm of linen ● Scissors ● Tracing paper ● Dressmaker's carbon ● Paintbrush ● Pébéo Setacolor opaque fabric paints in cherry 50, Oriental red 23, fawn 52, moss green 28 and green-gold 55 ● Pins ● Thread.

METHOD

Cut out the following pieces from the linen, adding a 1 cm seam allowance to all sides: 2 rectangles 40 x 35 cm (for the front and back of the bag), 2 rectangles 40 x 12 cm and one 35 x 12 cm (for the gusset). Cut 2 strips 42 x 8 cm (for the handles).

Transfer the fruit motifs on page 119 onto the RS of the large linen rectangle using dressmaker's carbon. Paint the redcurrants using a mixture of cherry and Oriental red and the gooseberries using a mixture of fawn and moss green. Add the veins on the fruits in fawn, cherry and moss green. For the shadows, mix green-gold and Oriental red. Leave the painted fabric to dry for 24 hours, then iron the back to fix the paints.

To make the bag, pin, then sew the front and back pieces to the side panels of the gusset, RS together. Sew the side panels to the front, bottom and back. Fold over the edge and topstitch around the bag. To make the handles, fold over 5 mm onto the WS around all sides of each handle strip and iron flat. Fold each strip in half lengthways with WS together and pin, then stitch together around all edges. Pin, then sew a handle to the inside edge of each side of the bag, next to the side seams.

To strengthen the bag, topstitch all the seams.

(see also page 119)

Shopping bags

SPORTY CHIC
Size: 40 x 30 cm

MATERIALS
**9 balls of Aran-weight yarn ●
1 pair of 6 mm knitting needles ●
1 cable needle ● 4 mm and 5 mm
crochet hooks ● 10 m of leather
cord ● 2 large yarn needles (for
threading the leather cord) ●
Heavy-duty sewing thread ●
45 cm of printed cotton (for the
lining) ● 2 leather handles.**

STITCHES USED
Knitting: stitch pattern
1st row: * slip 2 st onto cable
needle, placed behind work, knit
2 st, then knit 2 from cable needle *.
Repeat from * to end.
2nd row and all even rows: purl.
3rd row: * knit 2 st,* slip 2 st onto
cable needle, place in front of work,
knit 2 st, then knit 2 from cable
needle *. Repeat from * to end.
5th row: Begin again at the 1st row.
Knit edge stitch: knit 1 st at each
end of every row.
Crochet: double crochet (see
page 118).
Sewing: saddle stitch (see method).

METHOD
Front and back (make 2): cast on
102 st and work in the stitch
pattern as described above,
working one knit edge stitch at
each end of work. Continue until
work measures 40 cm. Cast off.
For the sides and bottom: cast on
34 st and work in the stitch pattern
as described, working 3 knit edge
stitches at each end of every row.
Continue until work measures
110 cm. Cast off.
Sew the side and bottom panel to
the front and back of the bag.
Highlight the edges with saddle
stitch using the leather cord: thread
each end of the cord into a needle.
Push one of the needles into the
side of the bag, at the top, bring it
out at the front, and pull until the
middle of the cord is between the 2
pieces. Insert the needle in a bit
lower down, from the front to the
side. Push the second needle into
the same holes but working in the
other direction, from the side to the
front. Continue, crossing the
needles into the same holes.

Edge the top of the bag with 2 rows
of double crochet.
Cut the lining from the printed
cotton (having first checked the
measurements against those of the
knitted bag): 2 rectangles of 43 x
33 cm and a band of 119 x 10 cm.
Sew the band to the front and back
rectangles, with RS together. Iron
open seams. Fold over 2 cm onto
the WS at the top edge and iron
flat. Turn RS out.
Slide the lining into the bag, WS
together, lining up the middle of the
sides and the edging. Sew the lining
to the top of the bag with heavy-
duty thread.
Fix the leather handles to the bag
on either side using leather cord.

Shopping bags

FRESHLY PICKED FLOWERS
Size: 28 x 35 cm

MATERIALS

30 cm of linen ● Scissors ● Photocopies of fresh flowers ● Soft gel gloss ● Soft paintbrush ● Rolling pin ● Sponge ● Heavy-duty sewing thread ● Pins.

METHOD

Cut out the pieces for the bag, following the template. Add a 1 cm seam allowance around each piece and 3 cm along each top edge.

To transfer images to bag, apply several coats of the soft gel gloss over the image with a paintbrush, being careful that it doesn't run over the edges. Place the coated side in position onto the fabric and burnish the image by rolling the rolling pin over the back, pressing down firmly, for at least 1 minute. Leave it to dry for 3 hours.

To remove the paper, soak a sponge in warm water, wring it out well, then rub it very gently over the paper. The little rolls of paper that will form will be easy to remove, while the printed image will remain stuck to the fabric.

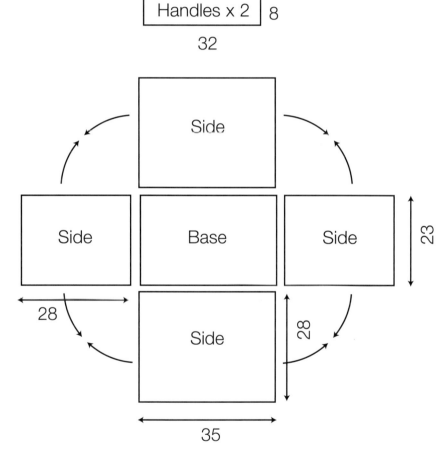

To make up the bag, sew the sides to the base, RS facing, then stitch corners and join the sides. Overstitch all seams. Fold over the top edges by 1 cm, then 3 cm, and iron flat.

Fold long edges of each handle into the middle, RS together, then fold in half lengthways to make a 2 cm-wide strip of 4 layers of fabric. Stitch down the lengths. Pin the ends of the handles inside the bag on either long side, spacing them 10 cm apart. Topstitch along the edge of the bag, removing pins along the way.

Shopping bags

OFF TO THE ORCHARD

MATERIALS
2 m of linen ● Sewing thread ● Scissors ● Pins ● Cardboard ● Metal letter and number stencils ● Fabric paint ● Stencil or paintbrush.

METHOD
Cut 2 rectangles each of 70 x 38 cm (for bag N° 3), 1 m x 22 cm (for bag N° 4) and 70 x 30 cm (for bag N° 7). Cut 3 rectangles 40 x 8 cm (for the handles).

For make bag N° 3, fold one of the large linen pieces in half to obtain a 38 x 35 cm rectangle. Iron the fold (which will be the middle of the base). With RS together, sew up the sides 1 cm in from the edges. Fold up the corners of the base fold by 8 cm and iron flat. Machine stitch along the fold and cut off the corners. This will create a 16 cm-wide gusset to the bag. Fold over 1 cm onto the WS around the top edge and iron flat.

Make up the lining in the same way with the other linen rectangle. Slip the lining into the bag with WS together.

Fold over 1 cm on each long edge of the handle strip, then fold in half lengthways, WS together. Stitch down each side. Cut the strip into 2 equal lengths and slip the ends of each handle between the bag and lining, pinning them in place. Stitch around the top of the bag, catching the ends of the handle into the seam as you go.

Make up bags N° 4 and N° 7 in the same way as bag N° 3.

To stencil the numbers onto the bags, fold the bag flat and slide a piece of cardboard inside to prevent the paint from soaking through onto the opposite side of the bag. Paint a number onto the middle of one side of the bag using the stencil and fabric paint. Allow to dry.

Storage

BEDDING BAGS

The 3 bags are shown clockwise from far right: large (checked), medium (blue) and small (floral print).

LARGE BAG
Size: 50 x 63 x 33 cm

MATERIALS
3 m of checked fabric ● Scissors ● Sewing thread ● 28 x 13.5 cm piece of denim ● 2 x 65 cm-long zips ● Pins.

METHOD
Cut 2 rectangles of 69 x 53 cm for the top and bottom of the bag, and 2 rectangles of 53 x 39 cm and 2 of 69 x 39 cm for the sides.
Overstitch the edges of all pieces, then fold over 1.5 cm and iron flat. Stitch the 4 side pieces together, RS facing, right at the edges, alternating long and short pieces. Stitch the bottom of the bag onto the sides in the same way. Iron open seams.
Stitch the top to the sides along one long edge and 13 cm of the way along the 2 shorter sides. Sew the fabric tapes of the zips along the other edges so that the 2 zip pullers meet in the middle of the long side. Turn the bag RS out.

To make the handle, fold over one long edge of the denim rectangle and iron flat. Fold lengthways in 3 to obtain a strip of 28 x 4 cm. Stitch along each long side. Fold over the ends of the handle and pin it in the middle of the zipped long side, centring it below the heads of the zips. Stitch the ends of the handle in place on the bag with a cross shape.

MEDIUM BAG
Size: 60 x 45 x 29 cm

MATERIALS
1.2 m of denim ● Scissors ● Sewing thread ● 2 x 65 cm-long zips ● Pins.

METHOD
Cut 2 rectangles of denim of 63 x 48 cm for the top and bottom of the bag, 2 rectangles of 48 x 32 cm and 2 of 63 x 32 cm for the sides, and 1 rectangle of 28 x 13.5 cm for the handle.
Make up the bag following the method given for the large bag.

SMALL BAG
Size: 50 x 40 x 15 cm

MATERIALS
1 m of floral cotton ● Scissors ● Sewing thread ● 28 x 13.5 cm piece of denim ● 2 x 55 cm-long zips ● Pins.

METHOD
Cut 2 rectangles of floral cotton of 53 x 43 cm for the top and bottom of the bag, 2 rectangles of 53 x 18 cm and 2 of 43 x 18 cm for the sides, and 1 rectangle of 28 x 13.5 cm for the handle.
Make up the bag following the method given for the large bag.

Storage

RECYCLED JEANS

MATERIALS
**The legs from 2 or 3 pairs of jeans
● Stiff card ● Scissors ● Stapler
● 10 m of thick blue plastic-
coated electrical wire ● Wire
cutters.**

METHOD
For the bottom of the basket, using
the template (1) on page 120, cut 2
pieces from the jeans and one in
stiff card, adding 1 cm all around
each fabric piece. Staple one of the
denim shapes to the card, folding
the excess over onto the back.

For the frame of the basket, cut a
95 cm length of the electrical wire.
Curve it around the cardboard
shape of the bottom of the basket.
Twist the ends together. Strengthen
the shape by crisscrossing 3
lengths across it (2). Cut 4 lengths
of the wire to the desired height of
the basket and cover them with
strips of the jeans sewn into tubes.
Form an oval from a 125 cm length
of the electrical wire and hook the
tops of the 4 wire lengths over its
edge and the bottoms over the
base shape (3).

To make the outside of the basket,
cut 2.5 x 35 cm strips from the
jeans. Cut 48 pieces from these
strips. Taper 22 of them to 1.5 cm at
one end (4). Lay the strips out next
to each other as follows: 6 tapered,
8 straight, 5 tapered, 5 straight,
6 tapered, 8 straight, 5 tapered and
5 straight. Stitch together along the
short end to obtain a long fringe (5).
Stitch the remaining strips of jeans
together lengthways to obtain a
long ribbon. Lay the fringe out on
a flat surface and weave the long
strips in and out of it, making sure
there are no gaps. Leave 10 cm
excess at each end. Continue
building up rows until you reach the
end of the strips. Close the basket
edges by hand sewing together the
ends of each horizontal strip.

Stitch the shape RS together
around the edge of the remaining
denim base shape.

Slide the frame inside the fabric
cover and fold the excess at the
top edge over onto the WS.
Topstitch along the edge. Slide the
denim-covered card base into the
bottom of the basket.

(see also page 120)

Storage

SEWING MACHINE COVER

MATERIALS

Tape measure ● Paper and pencil ● 1 m of striped cotton ● Scissors ● 1 m of iron-on interfacing ● Tracing paper ● Dressmaker's carbon ● Gold, fuchsia and white fabric paints ● Heavy-duty sewing thread ● Needle ● Bias binding (optional).

METHOD

Make a pattern for the cover by adapting the template on page 121 to the dimensions of your sewing machine. Cut out the number of pieces indicated, adding a 1 cm seam allowance all around each pattern piece and 3 cm for the lower hem. Cut out the same in the interfacing and iron this onto the back of each cotton piece.

Enlarge the daisies on page 121 and transfer them to the fabric using dressmaker's carbon. Add more at the bottom edges, fewer towards the top.

Paint the daisies with the fabric paints. Use yellow mixed with a tiny bit of fuchsia for the centres (add some highlights with a touch of white mixed with yellow). Paint the petals in white with pale pink tips, or in pale pink with fuchsia tips. Leave the paint to dry then iron on the back to fix the colours. Cut a slit for the sewing machine handle in the middle of the top piece, ending in a triangle at either end. Fold the fabric edges over onto the WS and machine stitch. Stitch the front and back pieces to the top, RS together. Iron open the seams. Stitch the sides to the front and back, RS together. Hem the bottom edge.

For a neater finish, you could cover the hems with a bias binding.

(see also page 121)

Storage

LAUNDRY BAGS
Size: 68 x 72 cm

MATERIALS
Electric drill ● 32 x 20 mm wooden lath: 4 lengths of 90 cm, 1 of 68 cm and 1 of 64 cm ● 25 mm-diameter dowel: 1 length of 68 cm and 1 of 64 cm ● Screwdriver ● 8 chipboard screws (3.5 x 40 mm) ● 2 flat-head bolts (5 x 50 mm) with washers and nuts ● 3 m of linen ● Scissors ● Sewing thread ● 1.3 m of Velcro® ● 8 mm-diameter thin dowel: 3 lengths of 19 cm ● Coloured fabric pens ● Pins.

METHOD
Drill a hole in the centre and 2.5 cm from each end of each 90 cm wooden lath. Screw the 68 cm length of 25 cm-diameter dowel between two 90 cm laths at the top. Screw the 68 cm lath across the bottom to create the outer frame. Make up the inner frame in the same way using the 64 cm lengths of dowel and lath. Bolt together the outer and inner frames through the centre holes to complete the wooden frame.

To make the laundry bags, cut out 3 of each of the pattern pieces on page 122. All the seams are sewn RS together 1 cm from the edges. Assemble the long sides of each piece to the next: A ⊦ D + B + E. Stitch in place around the bottom piece, F. Hem the top.

The tops of A and B will be turned back over the dowels to hold the bags in place. Sew a strip of one side of the Velcro® to the top edge of A and B on the WS. Sew the other strips of Velcro® to the inside of A and B at the level of the top of D and E.

Rectangle C will act as a cover flap. Fold the edges under and sew all the way around. Fold then sew a 3.5 cm hem at one end of C. Slide a 19 cm length of thin dowel into this channel. Close the ends. Using a fabric pen, draw the design onto the top of this flap, 32 cm from the edge. Mount the bag on the frame. Mark the fold of the fabric on the dowel with pins then remove the bag from the frame and sew the cover flap on the RS, 1 cm below the fold.

Cut 2 strips of linen 1 m x 12 cm. Fold over 1 cm on all edges and iron flat. Fold the strips lengthways, with WS together, and stitch down the length and across the ends. Sew a piece of Velcro® at each end of both strips so that they can be closed in a circle around the lower struts to hold the frame firm.

Assign a different colour to each temperature and mark clothes labels in felt tip with a diamond of the same colour. Your children will then be able to sort their laundry into the bags themselves!

(see also page 122)

Storage

ARMCHAIR TIDY

MATERIALS
Tape measure ● **Paper and pencil** ● **Medium-weave linen (for the base)** ● **Fine weave (for the pockets)** ● **8 cm-wide upholstery webbing (calculate amounts by measuring your armchair, see method)** ● **Scissors** ● **Heavy-duty sewing thread** ● **2 leather straps.**

METHOD
Adjust the pattern on page 123 according to the measurements of your armchair. A = the length of the arms; B = depth of the arms (measure on the inside from top to bottom of the chair); C = width of the armchair (measure below the seat cushion). Cut 2 rectangles A/B/B from the medium-weave linen, adding a 3 cm seam allowance on all edges. Fold over all edges by 5 mm, then by 2.5 cm, and iron flat. Sew a double hem along the edge and along the fold. To make pocket 1: cut a 50 x 29 cm rectangle of fine linen. Fold one side over by 1 cm, then another 1 cm, and iron flat. Sew along the edge of the hem and along the fold.

Iron a 1 cm turning on the other 3 sides then fold and iron a 3 cm-deep gusset at the top of each side. For the flap, cut a 40 x 16 cm rectangle. Fold over and sew a double hem on all sides as on the top of the pocket. Sew on the straps – one half on the pocket, the other half on the flap. Sew the pocket in place; first the top by opening the gussets, then the bottom by closing the gussets. Sew the flap just above.

To make pocket 2, cut a 29 x 23 cm rectangle. Fold and then double sew a 1 cm double flap at the top of the pocket. Fold over 1 cm on the other 3 edges and iron flat. Sew in place onto the panel on the inside of the other arm flap.

To make pocket 3, cut a 42 x 29 cm rectangle and assemble as for pocket 2. Sew it on the outside opposite pocket 2.

Join the 2 halves of the armchair tidy by firmly sewing the 2 pieces of webbing (C) between them. Position the armchair tidy on your armchair by placing these straps beneath the seat cushion.

(see also page 123)

Storage

SADDLEBAGS

Size: 37 x 78 cm (width x total length)

MATERIALS

3 m of red, white and blue striped upholstery fabric ● Scissors ● Heavy-duty sewing thread ● Safety pin ● 4 grommets ● Grommet kit ● Hammer or mallet ● 4 D-rings ● 1.2 m of cord ● Blue and red embroidery cotton ● Dressmaker's chalk.

METHOD

Cut out the pattern pieces on page 124 in the upholstery fabric, adding a 1 cm seam allowance around each piece and 2 cm at the top of pieces A and B for the top hems. For the buckle straps, cut 2 strips of 17 x 9 cm and 2 of 9 x 8 cm. Overstitch around the edge of each fabric piece. D = back of the saddlebags, A and B = saddlebags, E = flaps.

Fold the strap pieces lengthways RS together. Stitch along the lengths. Iron flat, placing the seam in the middle of the underside. Stitch the end of each of the long straps into a point and trim the seam allowance. Attach a safety pin to turn RS out. Fold over the other end of these long straps onto the WS (seamed side) and iron flat. Sew one to the bottom third of each of the A pieces as shown on the template.

To make each saddlebag, stitch a B piece on either side of A. Fold over and stitch a hem of 2 cm across the top of B/A/B. Stitch C to the bottom of A.

With RS together, fold D in half so that it measures 39 x 81 cm. Stitch sides together, leaving a small opening. Turn RS out and sew the opening closed.

Lay the 2 saddlebags RS to WS of D and stitch around the edges. Turn RS out.

Using dressmaker's chalk, draw your family name onto the front of one pocket flap (E). Embroider it in red and blue satin stitch.

To make the pocket flaps, lay the 2 E pieces RS together. Thread one of the short straps through 2 D-rings rings, fold in half widthways and slip the 2 ends between the E pieces along the middle of one short edge. Repeat on the other side of the flap.

Stitch around the edges, leaving an opening. Turn RS out. Neatly hand sew up the opening.

Stitch E to the base of saddlebags, placing it WS to RS of D. Fix the 4 grommets onto the centre of E/D, about 10 cm apart, as shown on the template.

Use the hole punch from the grommet kit to punch 4 holes on the centre of E/D as shown on the template, spacing them about 10 cm apart. Position the grommet on the tool and poke through one of the holes. Position the matching grommet piece over the first piece and use the hammer or mallet to join the 2 pieces. Repeat with the others. Cut the cord into 2 equal lengths and thread them through the eyelets to tie the saddlebags to the luggage rack of a bicycle.

(see also page 124)

Storage

LOG BASKET
Size: 45 x 55 cm

MATERIALS
1.2 m of burlap ● Heavy-duty sewing thread ● 80 cm of 8 cm-wide upholstery webbing ● Pins.

METHOD
Cut 2 squares of 59 cm and 8 rectangles of 59 x 49 cm.

With RS facing, sew the short sides of 4 rectangles together, 2 cm in from the edges, to make the sides of the bag. Stitch a square piece to the bottom of the sides, with RS together. Repeat with the other 4 rectangles and square to make the lining, this time leaving an opening of 20 cm in the middle of one seam. Cut the webbing into 2 equal lengths. Pin the ends of one length 12 cm apart on the WS of the top of the bag. Pin the ends of the other handle on the opposite side.

Slip the bag into the lining RS together and stitch around the top, catching the handles into the seam and removing the pins as you go. Turn the bag RS out through the hole in the lining. Sew up the lining. Topstitch around the top of the bag.

Diagrams & templates

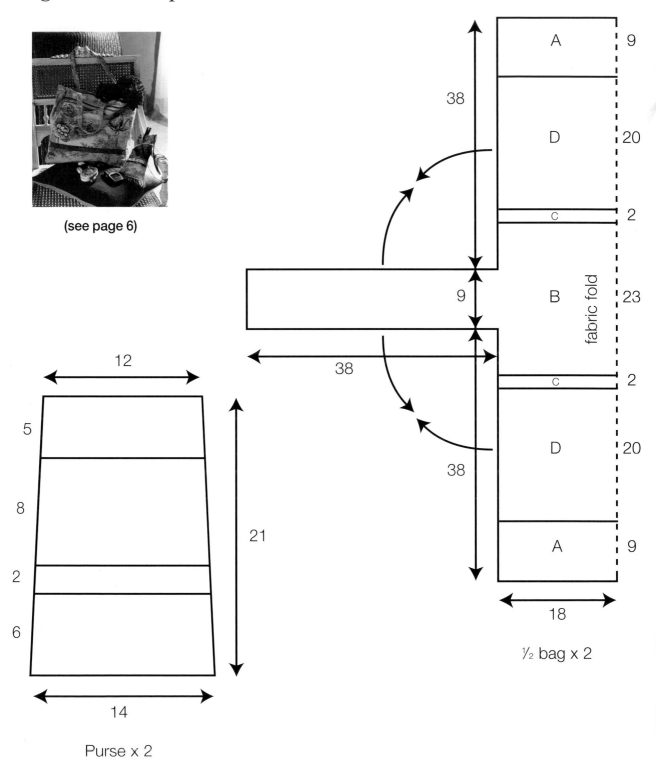

(see page 6)

A — 9

38

D — 20

c — 2

9 — B — fabric fold — 23

38

c — 2

D — 20

38

A — 9

18

½ bag x 2

12

5

8

21

2

6

14

Purse x 2

Design to scale

Diagrams & templates

(see page 12)

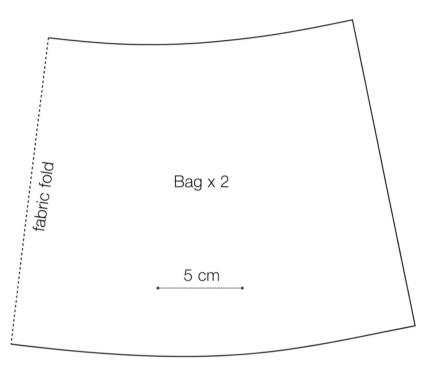

fabric fold

Bag x 2

5 cm

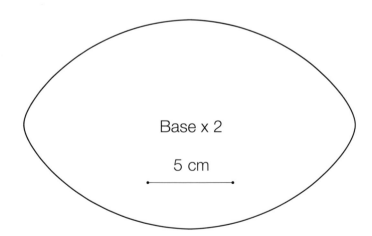

Base x 2

5 cm

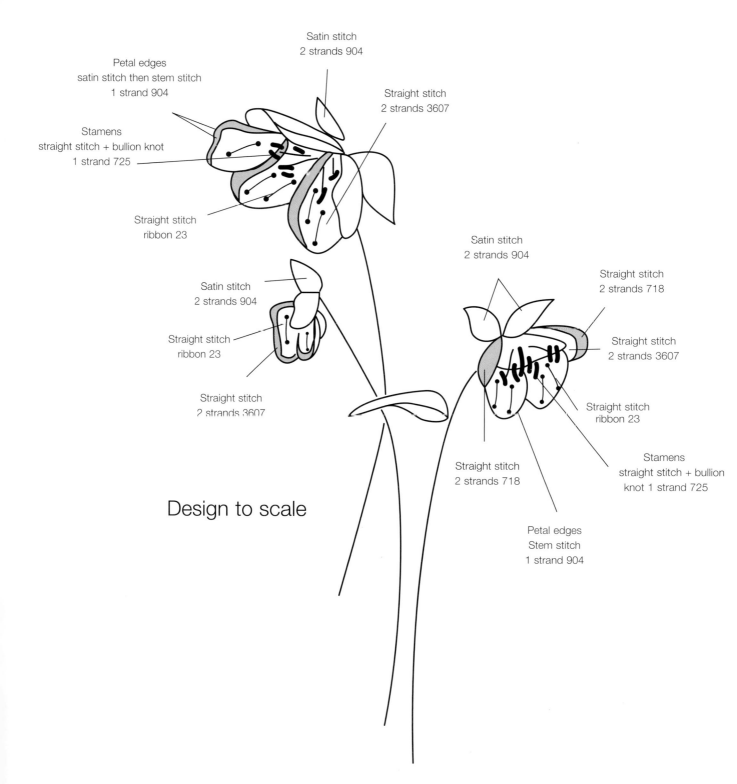

Satin stitch
2 strands 904

Petal edges
satin stitch then stem stitch
1 strand 904

Straight stitch
2 strands 3607

Stamens
straight stitch + bullion knot
1 strand 725

Straight stitch
ribbon 23

Satin stitch
2 strands 904

Straight stitch
ribbon 23

Straight stitch
2 strands 3607

Design to scale

Satin stitch
2 strands 904

Straight stitch
2 strands 718

Straight stitch
2 strands 3607

Straight stitch
ribbon 23

Stamens
straight stitch + bullion
knot 1 strand 725

Straight stitch
2 strands 718

Petal edges
Stem stitch
1 strand 904

Diagrams & templates

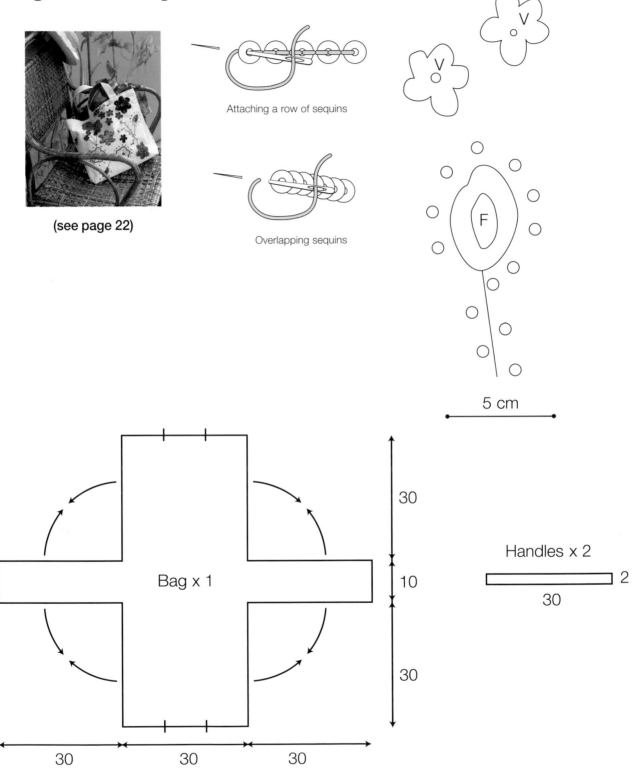

(see page 22)

Attaching a row of sequins

Overlapping sequins

V

V

F

5 cm

Bag x 1

30

10

30

30

30

30

Handles x 2

2

30

L = leaves

V = velvet flowers

C = clover leaves

R = rosebuds

S = sequins

B = beads

Diagrams & templates

(see page 28)

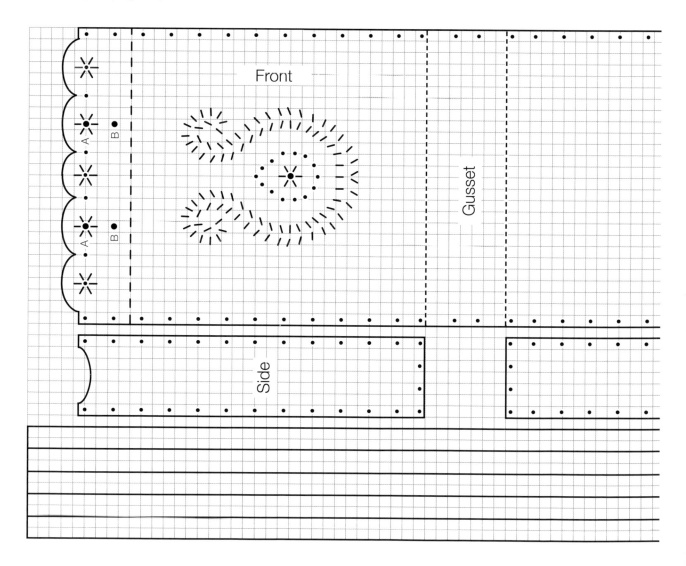

1 square = 1 cm^2

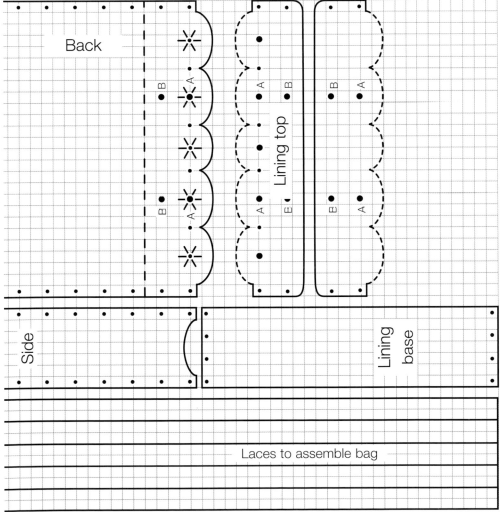

Back

Side

Lining top

Lining base

Laces to assemble bag

Diagrams & templates

(see page 30)

Ribbon rose

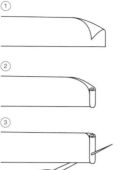

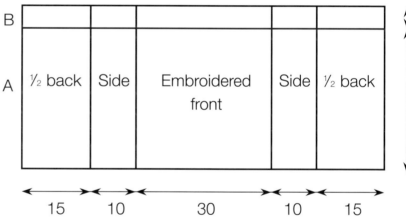

B						5
A	½ back	Side	Embroidered front	Side	½ back	31

15	10	30	10	15

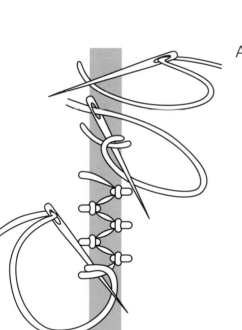

5 mm

Knotted herringbone
insertion stitch

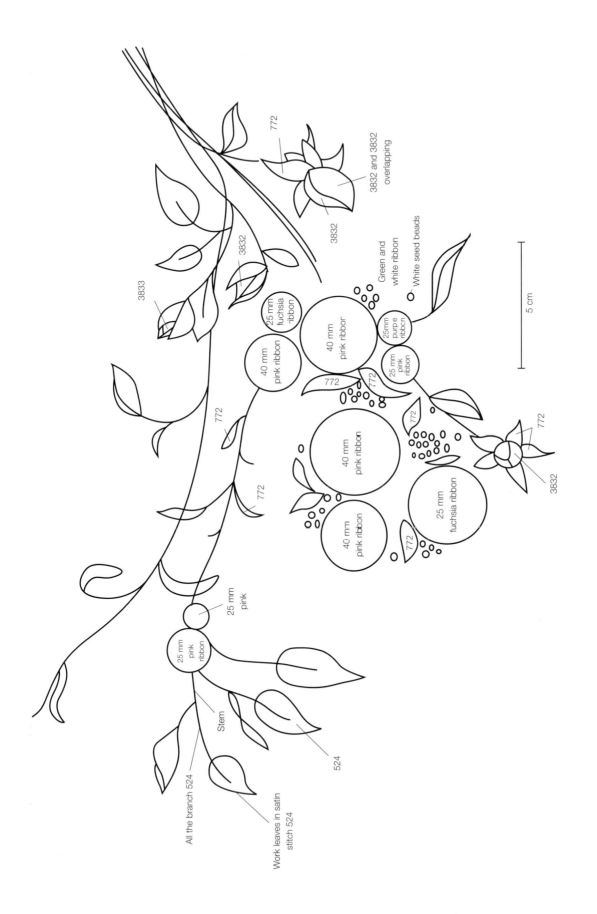

772

3832 and 3832 overlapping

3832

Green and
white ribbon

White seed beads

3833

3832

25 mm
fuchsia
ribbon

25mm
purple
ribbon

40 mm
pink ribbon

40 mm
pink ribbon

25 mm
pink
ribbon

772

772

772

772

772

40 mm
pink ribbon

3832

772

772

40 mm
pink ribbon

25 mm
fuchsia ribbon

772

40 mm
pink ribbon

25 mm
pink

25 mm
pink
ribbon

Stem

524

All the branch 524

Work leaves in satin
stitch 524

5 cm

Diagrams & templates

(see page 36)

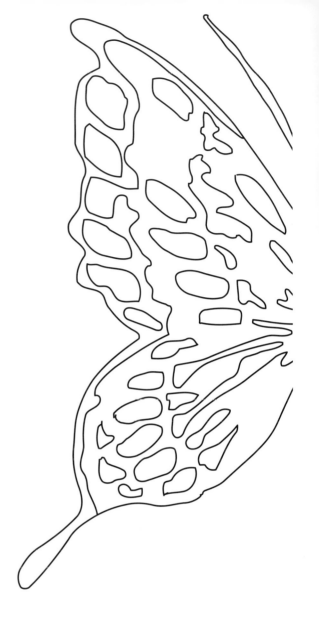

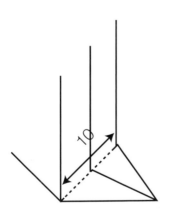

Detail of gusset fold

5 cm

Diagrams & templates

(continued from page 42)

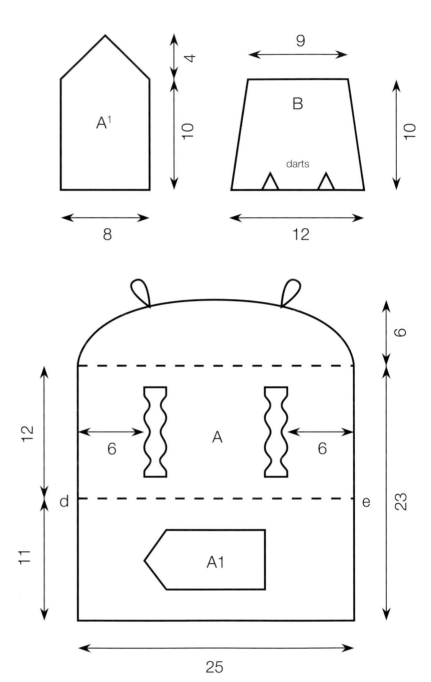

To make the body of the bag, fold over onto the WS, iron flat and stitch a 1 cm hem on edge bc of piece D, de of piece E, de of piece F, and fg of piece K. Turn over 1 cm onto the WS of all non-hemmed edges of these pieces and iron flat. Pin then sew all non-hemmed edges of pieces D, E, F and K to C, WS together, fixing 2 elastic loops into the top rounded edge.

Sew the side panels (GI and HJ) to E, RS together, then sew them, RS facing, to the sides of D and F, starting at the bottom. The extra piece at the top will fold over the bag's contents.

To make the straps, cut 2 strips of 100 x 5 cm (+ seam allowance) in checked fabric. Place WS of strips together and pin cotton fleece to them. Sew along edges, removing pins, and leave one side open. Turn RS out. Close the opening and topstitch edge. Pins strap ends to the sides of the bag. Sew the straps with a square of stitching, sewing an 'X' through the centre from corner to corner for extra strength. Sew buttons onto the front of the bag to line up with the elastic loops. Cut pattern pieces D, E, F and K (less 5 mm on each side) in thin card or plastic. Slip these pieces between the 2 fabric layers. Add a few stitches along fg and hk on the top flap (K) to keep the card in place.

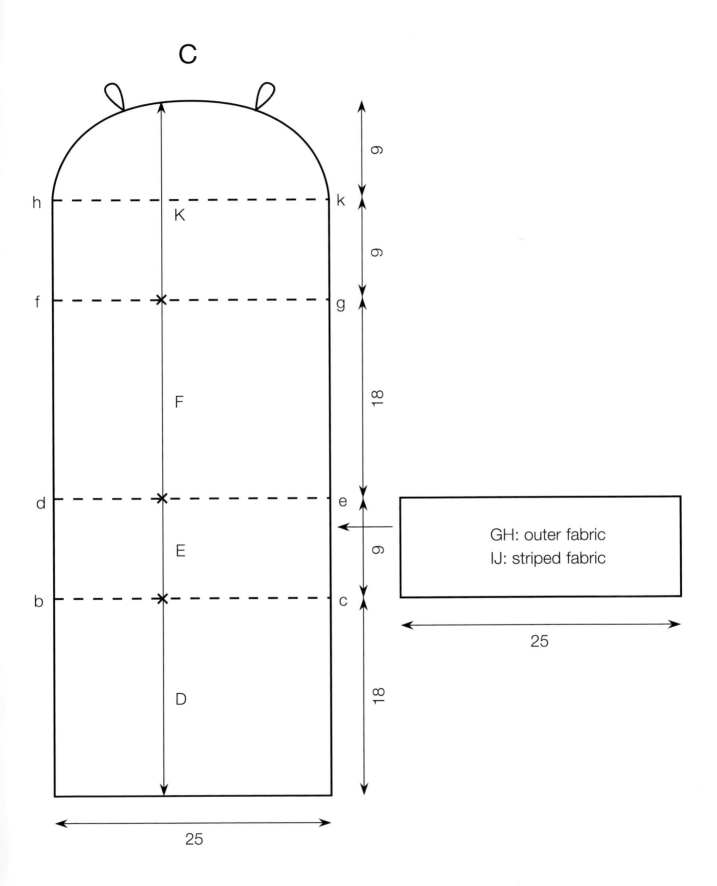

C

h · · · · · · k

K

f · · · ✕ · · · g

F

d · · · ✕ · · · e

E

b · · · ✕ · · · c

D

9

9

18

9

18

25

GH: outer fabric
IJ: striped fabric

25

Diagrams & templates

(see page 44)

BROWNS
3371 = a
938 = b
801 = c
300 = d

BEIGES
612
613 = ●
822 = ○
3822
3823 = :

GREENS
733 = e
166 = f
3819 = g
165 = i

ORANGES
728
783

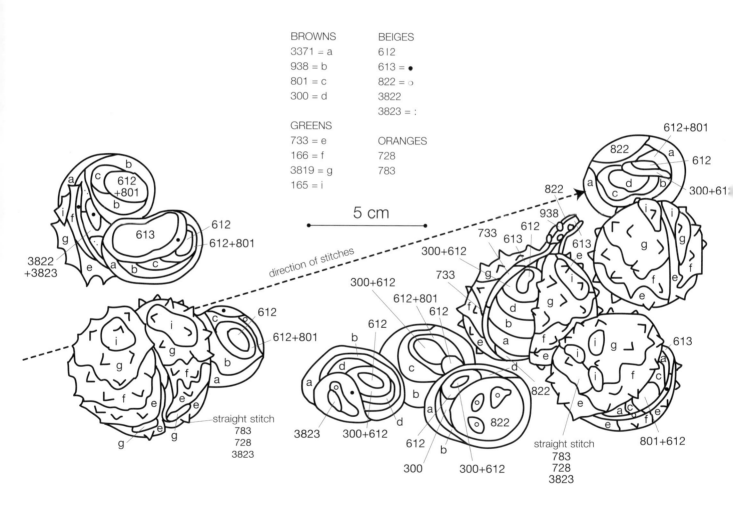

5 cm

direction of stitches

612+801
822
a
612
822
d
b
938
300+61
733
612
a
c
612
613
300+612
613
i
i
733
e
g
g
g
g
300+612
f
d
f
e
612+801
g
612
f
e
b
e
612
a
b
a
e
e
613
d
c
i
i
i
g
b
d
f
c
a
822
e
f
822
f
e
e
a c
e
d
f e
612
b
822
801+612
3823
300+612
o
612
b
straight stitch
783
728
3823
300
300+612

612
+801
613
612
612+801
3822
+3823
e
g
f
i
a
b
c
b
c
a
b
a

612
i
c
o
612+801
g
i
b
g
a
f
e
f
e
e
e
g
g
straight stitch
783
728
3823

(continued from page 52)

METHOD

Using the template below, cut the patterns in each fabric, adding 1 cm seam allowance around each piece. For the handles, cut 2 strips of printed fabric 12 cm wide and of the desired length (to hold in the hand or on the shoulder). Fold them in half lengthways with RS facing. Sew the edges together 1 cm in from the edge. Turn RS out and iron flat. Topstitch along both sides.

With RS together, sew the ends to the front and back, as shown on the template, stitching 1 cm in from the edges.

Pin the handles to the top of the bag, one on each side, spacing them about 12 cm apart.

Sew one of the top (B) pieces to the top edge of the front. Fold over 1 cm on all 3 open sides of the top and around the top edges of the bag and iron flat. Tack one tape of the zip under the edge of one top piece and the other tape to the other top edge piece.

Make up another bag in the same way. Slide it into the first one, WS together. Sew around the top of the bag, stitching through all 3 layers – bag exterior, zip and lining.

LAUNDRY BAG
Size: 46 x 40 cm

MATERIALS
70 cm of floral fabric ● Scissors ● Sewing thread ● Safety pin.

METHOD

Cut 2 rectangles of 43 x 59 cm for the front and back of the bag. Fold over 1.5 cm around all edges and iron flat. Fold over the top edge of back and front piece by 10 cm, RS together, and iron flat. Starting from the top, sew 7 cm down each side, 1.5 cm from the edge. Turn RS out. Sew across this fold 7 cm from the top, then 3 cm lower down, to create a drawstring channel. Repeat with the back.

For the loops at the bottom through which the straps will pass, cut 2 rectangles of 12 x 8 cm. Fold them lengthways RS together and stitch along the length 1 cm in from the edge. Turn RS out. Fold them in half and pin them on the RS of the lower corners of 1 side (the back). Lay the back and front pieces, RS together, and sew the 3 sides together from just below 1 of the top hems to the other, 1.5 cm in from the edges, catching the loops into the seam at the bottom corners. To make the stitching easier, snip 1.5 cm into the side hem just under the top hem.

To make the 2 long straps, cut 2 fabric strips of 200 x 8 cm. Fold over a small strip down each of the long sides and iron flat. With RS together, fold each strip in half lengthways and sew along the length near the edge.

Slide a strap through the top hem, then through one of the loops. Knot the ends together. Repeat with the other strap on the opposite side.

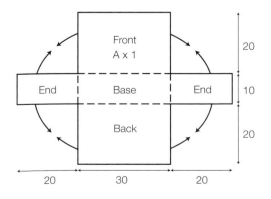

Diagrams & templates

(see page 54)

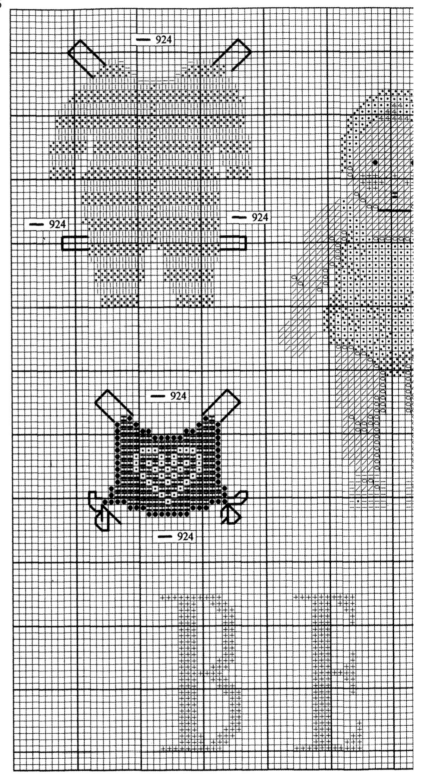

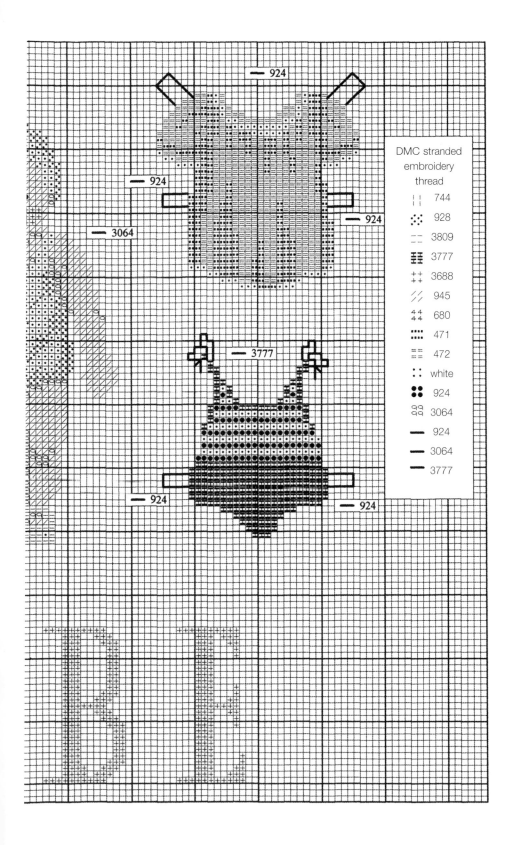

Diagrams & templates

(see page 56)

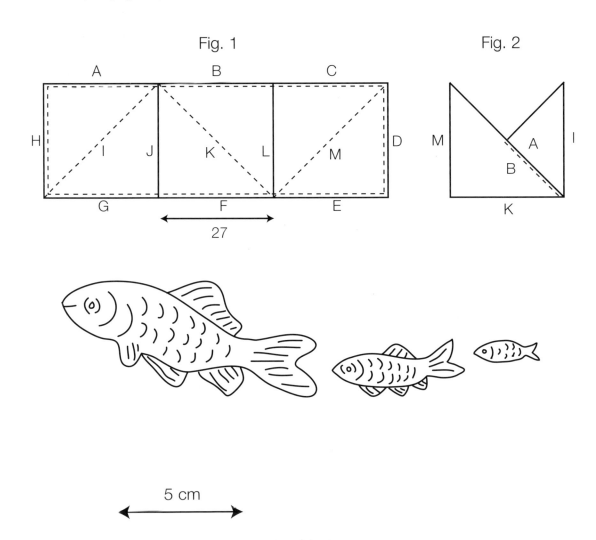

Fig. 1   Fig. 2

5 cm

(see page 58)

Handles (32 × 4) × 2

Bag (23 × 20)
x 2

Muzzle
x 1

Nose
x 1

Eye
x 2

Badge x 1

Body
x 1

5 cm

Diagrams & templates

(see page 62)

Coccinelle demoiselle
bête à bon Dieu,
Coccinelle demoiselle
monte jusqu'aux cieux
Petits points blancs
elle attend,
Petits points rouges
elle bouge,
Petits points noirs
Coccinelle au revoir.

light green

dark green

5 cm

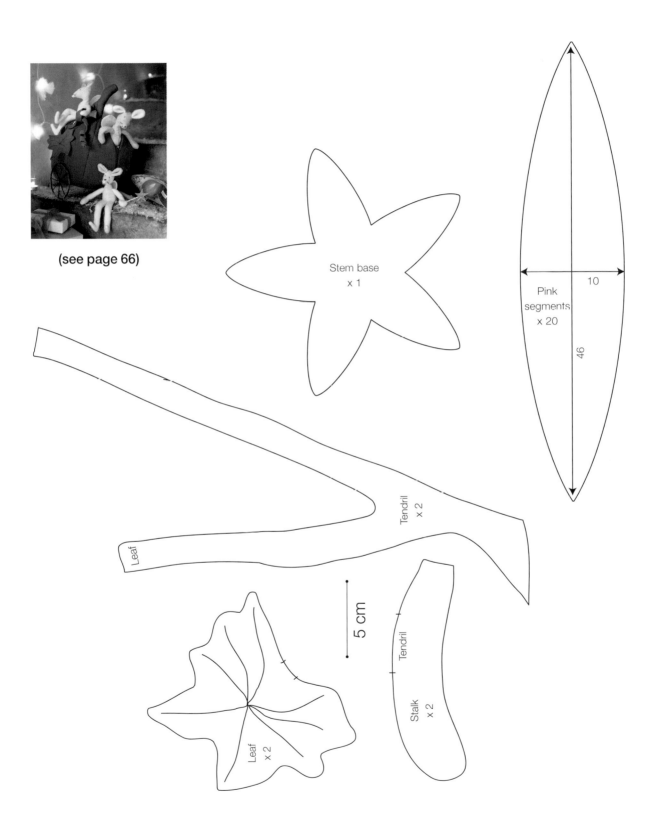

(see page 66)

Stem base
x 1

Pink
segments
x 20

10

46

Leaf

Tendril
x 2

5 cm

Leaf
x 2

Tendril

Stalk
x 2

Diagrams & templates

(see page 70)

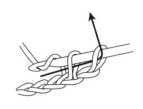

1

2

3

4

Double crochet

3

row 2

raffia

row 1

⬭ Chain stitch

✕ Double crochet

⬭ = 4 treble crochets joined together

(see page 74)

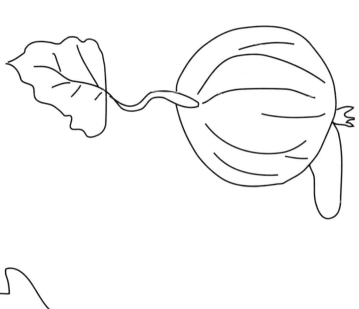

119

Diagrams & templates

(see page 84)

 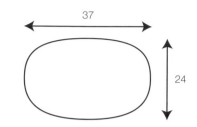
37

24

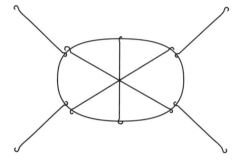

④ 1.5 | Tapered strip | 2.5

⑤
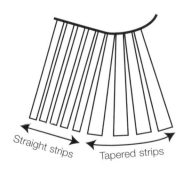

Straight strips   Tapered strips

(see page 86)

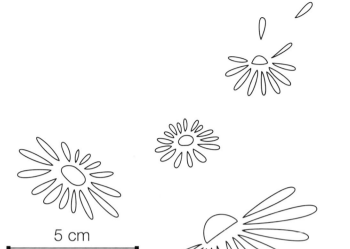

5 cm

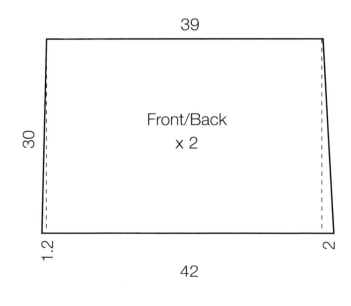

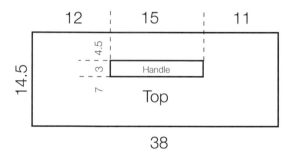

12   15   11

4.5

3   Handle

7

Top

14.5

38

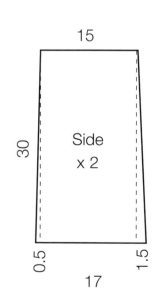

15

30

Side
x 2

0.5   1.5

17

39

30

Front/Back
x 2

1.2   2

42

Diagrams & templates

(see page 88)

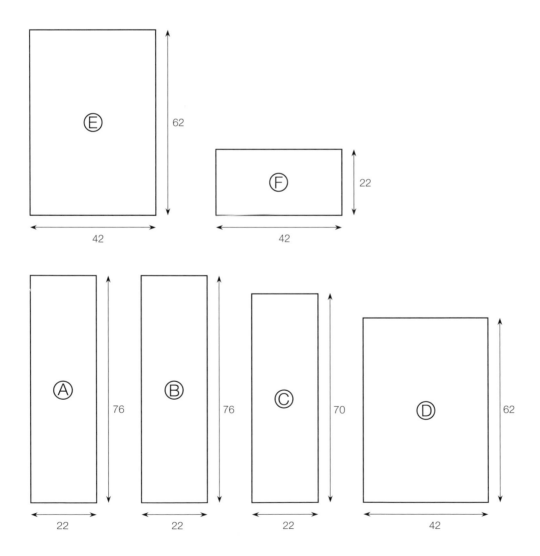

E 62 42

F 22 42

A 22 76

B 22 76

C 22 70

D 42 62

(see page 90)

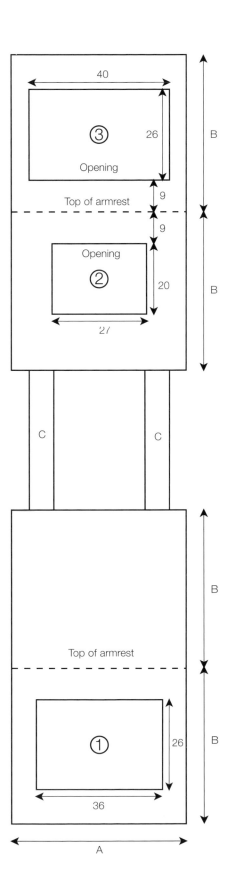

40

③
Opening

26

B

9

Top of armrest

9

Opening
②

20

27

B

C   C

B

Top of armrest

B

①

26

36

B

A

Diagrams & templates

(see page 92)

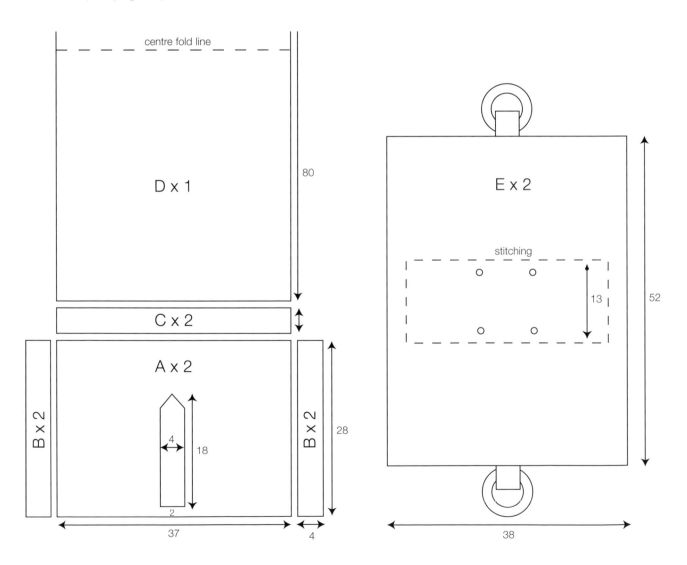

centre fold line

D x 1

80

C x 2

A x 2

B x 2

B x 2

28

4

18

2

37

4

E x 2

stitching

13

52

38

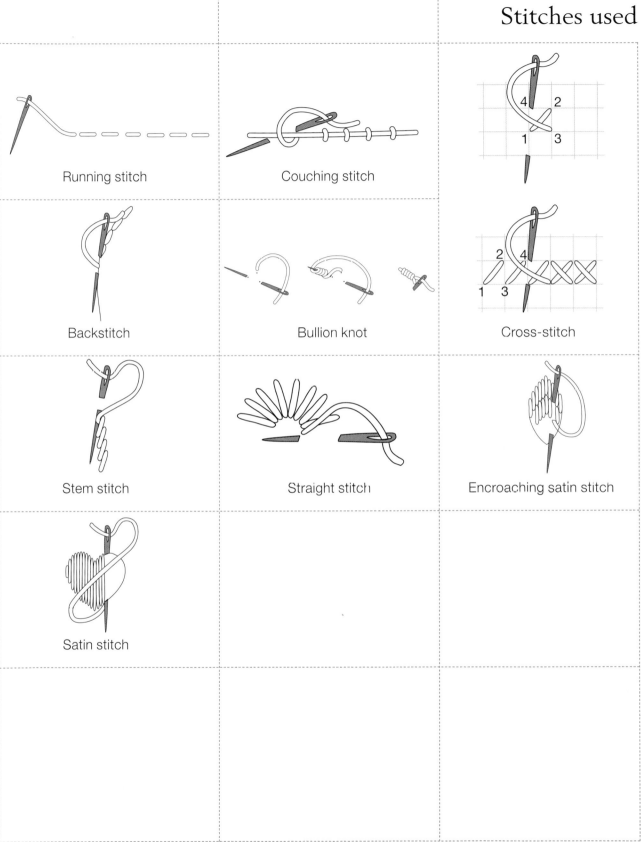

Stitches used

Running stitch

Couching stitch

Backstitch

Bullion knot

Cross-stitch

Stem stitch

Straight stitch

Encroaching satin stitch

Satin stitch

Index

Credits

PHOTOGRAPHERS

Jean-Claude Amiel (p. 51), Sylvie Becquet (pp. 25, 27), Juliette D'Assay (pp. 43, 45, 55, 59, 71, 87), Gilles De Chabaneix (pp. 23, 33, 53, 57, 81, 85), Patrice Degrandry (p. 35), Christophe Dugied (pp. 7, 9, 11, 13, 17, 19, 21, 29, 37, 65, 67), Louis Gaillard (pp. 15, 31, 41, 49, 61, 63, 69, 75, 77, 79, 83, 89), Guillaume Girardot (p. 39), Sylvie Lancrenon (pp. 47, 91, 95), Bernard Maltaverne (p. 93), Yoichiro Sato (p. 73).

DESIGNERS

Marie-France Annasse (p. 61), Charlotte Bailly (p. 9), Blandine Boyer (pp. 79, 85), Eve-Marie Briolat (pp. 11, 45), Sabine Cano (p. 75), Pascale Chombart de Lawe (pp. 41, 83), Catherine Coget (pp. 13, 31), Corinne Crasbercu (p. 19), Ayako Kawauchi David (p. 57), Anaïk Descamps (p. 73), Caroline Diaz (pp. 7, 35), Céline Dupuy (p. 21), Christl Exelmans (p. 65), Michiru Fuji (p. 29), Florence Guinet (p. 51), Élodie Hamon (pp. 39, 49), Dalila Ladjal (p. 67), Joy Laguenie (p. 43), Irène Lassus (p. 37), Sophie Lecornu (p. 59), Véronique Méry (pp. 23, 33, 47, 53, 69, 81, 91, 95), Lise Meunier (p. 63), Anne Muchir (p. 55), Magali Ogier (p. 89), Dany Ribaillet (p. 77), Nathalie Spiteri (p. 71), Marion Taslé (p. 87), Dominique Turbé (pp. 15, 17, 25, 27), Cécile Vessière (p. 93).

MAKERS

Eve-Marie Briolat (pp. 11, 45), Pascale Chombart de Lawe (pp. 15, 25, 27, 41, 47, 57, 71, 77, 83, 89, 91, 95), Catherine De Chabaneix (pp. 23, 33, 53, 57, 81, 85), Christl Exelmans (pp. 31, 65), Marion Faver (p. 93), Élodie Hamon (pp. 39, 49), Caroline Lancrenon (p. 61), Françoise Lapeyre (p. 73), Vania Leroy (pp. 43, 63, 67, 75, 87), Véronique Méry (pp. 69, 79), Camille Soulayrol (pp. 7, 9, 13, 17, 21, 35, 51, 59), Maïté Thiébaut-Morelle (p. 17), Dominique Turbé (pp. 19, 29, 55), Marianne Voituriez (p. 37).